W9-DBX-748

PARIS
in your pocket

MICHELIN
Travel Publications

MANUFACTURE FRANÇAISE DES PNEUMATIQUES MICHELIN

Place des Carmes-Déchaux – 63000 Clermont-Ferrand (France)

© Michelin et Cie. Propriétaires-Éditeurs 1996

Dépôt légal Avril 96 – ISBN 2-06-6630201-5 – ISSN 1272-1689

No part of this publication may be reproduced in any form

without the prior permission of the publisher.

Printed in Spain 01-02/6

MICHELIN TRAVEL PUBLICATIONS
Hannay House
39 Clarendon Road
WATFORD Herts WD17 1JA - UK
☎ (01923) 205240
www.ViaMichelin.com

MICHELIN TRAVEL PUBLICATIONS
Michelin North America
One Parkway South
GREENVILLE, SC 29615
☎ 1-800 423-0485
www.ViaMichelin.com

CONTENTS

INTRODUCTION

A boat trip along the Seine provides excellent views of some of the main attractions in Paris.

Paris – the name invokes a vision, a feeling, which no other city can equal. For many, Paris is a symbol of cultural sophistication; the arts – opera, dance, music, sculpture and painting – are honoured here to an extent almost unique. For others, the city stands as a beacon of freedom and democracy, while for others Paris spells romance, a city of lovers and life, and the delights of food and drink.

The thrill of Paris is that all this is true. Each of us can find here a Paris to delight. The theatres, galleries and museums are without equal for their sheer number and richness.

The city is unique in its welcome to the visitor, too. Paris, remarkably small for a city of such renown, offers a diversity that guarantees to meet the expectations of every visitor. It is large enough to possess the great buildings and grand vistas of a capital of outstanding international importance, and yet it harbours and cherishes local neighbourhoods where native Parisians live, shop, eat, drink and play and where over 2 000 years of history flavour today's reality.

Yet this rich diversity can be explored so easily by the visitor. The city can be crossed by RER train in 30 minutes. A two-hour stroll will take you from the Ile St-Louis in the east to the Eiffel Tower in the west, with time to pause and admire everything on the way, so every visitor to the city can leave with a lasting memory of the real Paris.

HOW TO USE THIS GUIDE

This guide is divided into four main sections:

Background introduces the history of Paris, tracing how the city we see today has evolved. Its rich art and culture, its heroes and legends, and the culture and people of Paris today are outlined.

Exploring Paris opens with a list of the top sights which should be on everyone's holiday checklist. The city is then divided into nine main areas and the reader is taken on a tour of each, highlighting the main sights and attractions, landmarks and points of interest. Sections on the *Major Museums* and *Other Museums* detail where you can see different aspects of Paris's rich history. *Further Afield* includes a selection of sights outside the city centre, and *Out of Town* suggests excursions outside Paris.

Enjoying Your Visit provides friendly, no-nonsense advice on day-to-day activities which can make the difference between a good holiday and a great one – eating out, shopping, sports and entertainment, as well as information about local festivals and the all-important factor – the weather!

A-Z Factfinder is an easy-to-use reference section packed with useful information, covering everything you may need to know on your visit, from tipping and hiring cars to using the telephone or buying stamps. A word of warning: opening hours and telephone numbers frequently change, so be sure to double check with a local tourist office when planning your visit.

The Champs-Élysées, illuminated with Christmas lights.

Plan your visit using the Michelin star ratings:
*** *Highly recommended*
** *Recommended*
* *Interesting*

HISTORY

The First Thousand Years

That Paris is the key to a vital region of western Europe was recognised by the conquering Romans. The Ile-de-France, the area embraced by the rivers Seine, Oise, Aisne, Ourcq and Marne, was crucial to their advance into northern Europe and remained so for those that followed.

When **Julius Caesar** arrived he found the Ile de la Cité occupied by a Celtic tribe, the **Parisii**. After their overthrow their settlement, Lutetia, was rebuilt by the Romans and became an important port.

Clovis made Paris his capital in 508 but it was under the Carolingians that real prosperity came. **Charlemagne**, grandson of Charles Martel, founder of the dynasty,

The ruins of the Roman baths comprise part of the Museum of the Middle Ages. The original vast bath complex was built by the Guild of Paris boatmen.

made his capital at Aix-la-Chapelle (Aachen), leaving the government of Paris to the Count and the control of much of its commerce to the great abbeys. After attack by the Norsemen, the Carolingian Empire broke up and it was not until Hugh Capet became king in 987 that Paris became a capital once more, and its position strengthened both politically and commercially.

The Middle Ages

It was the reign of Philip II, **Philippe Auguste** (1180–1223), that lifted Paris to supremacy in European civilization. The charter of the University of Paris was approved by this great monarch, and Les Halles was created to give merchants a covered area in which to trade. A fortress

One of the magnificent rose windows in the Notre-Dame Cathedral.

and palace (the early Louvre) was built next to the Church of St-Germain-l'Auxerrois and work on the great Cathedral of Notre-Dame was pushed forward, but it was Philip's wall that defined and secured the city. Some of it can be seen today in the Marais opposite the St-Paul Village, and elsewhere.

The legacy of **Louis IX**, St Louis (1226–70), is yet more inspiring. Pious in the extreme, he built a chapel for his personal use – Sainte-Chapelle – within the precincts of the royal palace on the Ile de la Cité. The first government archive and library was also his creation and Louis's support for scholarship encouraged the growth of the university that became known as the Sorbonne.

The **Hundred Years' War** (1337–1453) brought the English to Paris. An alliance with the Burgundians gave them access to the city when the Armagnacs were ejected in 1418, and they ruled until Charles VII threw them out (1436).

A Town Becomes a City

The Renaissance found **François I** (1515–47) its great ally. He brought Benvenuto Cellini, Leonardo da Vinci and the like to the kingdom, made Budé master of the royal library and thus laid the foundation of the Bibliothèque Nationale, and encouraged the growth of the university and a degree of freedom of speech. But the shadow of religious dispute was soon to fall across this glowing scene. In 1534 Ignatius Loyola and Francis Xavier founded the Society of Jesus – the Jesuits – in the crypt of the church marking the martyrdom of St Denis at 11 Rue Yvonne-le-Tac, (Montmartre), and the quarrel between

The Palace of Justice, on the Ile de la Cité, is the heart of the civil and judicial system.

Catholics and Protestants eventually boiled over into the **Wars of Religion**.

On 23 August 1572 the St Bartholemew's Day Massacre heralded the beginning of a 15-year civil war. When **Henry IV** seized the throne in 1589 the Catholic League was horrified at the prospect of a Protestant monarch. Paris refused the king entry and suffered a siege which reduced the people of the city to eating anything that moved. Finally, the threat of intervention by the Spanish forced Henry to withdraw and it became clear his throne would never be secure unless he became a Catholic. In 1593 he was received into the Catholic church. 'Paris is worth a mass,' he said.

Rebuilding

A frenzy of building subsequently overtook the capital. The Louvre was remodelled, the Place Dauphine and the Place Royale (now the Place des Vosges) built and a bridge uncluttered with houses constructed across the Seine, the Pont Neuf.

Henry's robust, cheerful and sociable character (he was known as 'Le Vert Galant' – the good ol' boy) attracted the rich and the aristocratic to the city and their *hôtels particuliers* were built in the Marais. The momentum of development even survived Henry's assassination by Ravaillac in 1610.

In 1611 **Louis XIII** licensed Christophe Marie to develop the islands that were united to form the Ile St-Louis, but the enterprise was dogged by bankruptcies and took years to complete.

The Place des Vosges, the city's oldest square, was constructed by Henry IV for ceremonies and festivals. It is surrounded by elegant houses and recently renovated gardens.

The Sun King

Louis XIV, the Sun King, came to the throne in 1643 but he neglected Paris. Fortunately, however, Jean-Baptiste Colbert, appointed finance minister in 1665, recognised the importance of Paris in the economic and cultural life of France. A classicist, he encouraged learning and the arts, he also overhauled the government. Business prospered, but the taxes needed to pay for this economic expansion and the king's ill-

advised wars were heavy and the contrast between rich and poor became even more extreme, with the wealth of the king epitomized in the building of Versailles. The face of the city was also transformed; the medieval wall was swept away and new avenues, such as the Champs-Élysées, appeared. The Place Vendôme was built by Hardouin-Mansart, and the theatre thrived with plays by Corneille, Racine and Molière.

Building continued under Louis XV (1715–74). The *hôtels* in the Faubourg St-Honoré and many in the Faubourg St-Germain date from this time, and the Age of Enlightenment, a European philosphical movement, brought forth Voltaire, Rousseau and Diderot.

The Revolution

By the 1780s **Louis XVI** and **Marie-Antoinette** found themselves on the brink of revolution. In 1789, 88 per cent of a Paris worker's income was needed to buy bread, and political unrest seethed. Riot and disorder spread until, on 14 July, a mob stormed the almost empty Bastille. After this symbolically important day, Paris once again led the French nation.

Complex events followed, but eventually the monarchy was overthrown. The Revolution was the creature of an unstable society, part led by the republicans, Danton, Robespierre and companions, and part driven by the mob. The king was tried under the name Louis Capet, and condemned to death by a vote of 387 to 334.

Some while before, Louis had approved a new method of execution based on a device invented in Halifax, England. A derivative of this, seen in Scotland by Dr Joseph Guillotin, was perfected by him, and on 21 January 1793 Louis verified its efficiency.

In September the mob demanded that 'the enemy within' be suppressed and the **Reign of Terror** (1793–4), the extreme phase of the Revolution during which some 3 000 people perished in Paris alone, began. The aristocrats and the dignified Marie-Antoinette went to the guillotine first, but soon anyone whom the revolutionary Tribunal wanted out of the way was to follow.

In the anti-religious fervour of the Revolution vast damage was done to the churches, abbeys and châteaux of the land, as well as to its people. A further attempt to use force to overthrow the government in 1795 was thwarted when a young artillery officer fired upon the crowd. His name was **Napoleon Bonaparte**.

The Empire

A new constitution was adopted in 1795 and Bonaparte became a member of the ruling triumvirate. He was appointed First Consul in 1799 and crowned Emperor on 2 December 1804 in Notre-Dame.

He granted Paris special status, placing it directly under his rule. In his determination to 'make Paris the capital of Europe', he launched numerous rebuilding projects. The Louvre Palace was altered; the Arc de Triomphe du Carrousel erected; new bridges (Austerlitz, Iéna, and the smaller Passerelle des Arts) were built across the Seine and others altered; and the Ourcq and St-Martin Canals were dug. The spoils of war enriched the artistic treasures of the Louvre. Roads were built, and everywhere monuments were raised to himself and his armies, including the Arc de Triomphe.

The Arc de Triomphe du Carrousel, built in honour of Napoleon Bonaparte, from 1806-8.

The **Restoration**, which brought **Louis XVIII** to the throne, in 1815, was marked by the addition of 21 000 apartment houses and many new streets, but little else except the concept of dining away from home; the restaurant was born.

In 1830, three days of revolution known as the 'Three Glorious Days' led to the overthrow of **Charles X**, brother of Louis XVI and Louis XVIII, and set **Louis-Philippe** on the throne. In 1840, the romance of Napoleonic memory was fed by the return of the Emperor's body to the Invalides, but Louis-Philippe failed to hold a balance in the face of inflation, unemployment and corruption in politics. In 1848 revolution struck again, and France once more became a republic.

The City of Light

Attempts to set up a new government were dogged by riot, and in June 1848 the National Guard slew some 4 000 workers in the Faubourg St-Antoine. Louis-Napoléon emerged as President and at the end of his term seized power as First Consul. His major

impact on Paris was in the appointment of Baron Haussmann to create an Imperial city, and Paris was dubbed the City of Light.

However, the severe defeat of the Franco-Prussian War in 1870 brought this to an end. In March 1871, after the armistice that ended the Franco-Prussian War, a minority of Parisians (left-wing Republicans and workers) felt betrayed by their leaders. They seized the cannons in Montmartre and set up the **Paris Commune**. The wealthy middle classes and the army fled the city. Two months later the revolt was cruelly crushed. The 'Bloody Week' left more than 20 000 dead among the insurrectionists. Thousands more were imprisoned or exiled to Devil's Island off the coast of French Guiana.

The *Belle Époque*

Paris was gradually rebuilt and Haussmann's schemes largely fulfilled. At the same time, one of the most extraordinary flowerings of the arts in European history took place. By the end of the 19C the names of artists such as Degas, Renoir, Monet, Seurat, Cézanne, Van Gogh, Picasso and Matisse were immortalized. Composers Debussy, Saint-Saëns and Bizet, and writers Zola and Mallarmé, were known worldwide.

The architectural delights of art nouveau and the raffish reputation of the city as a sensual playground were manifest. The international fairs of 1889 (which produced the Eiffel Tower) and 1900 proclaimed France's burgeoning commercial and industrial growth.

Modern Paris

The pre-eminence of Paris as a tourist destination was established after the First

The Kiss, by Auguste Rodin, is housed in the Rodin Museum.

World War. There had always been plenty of visitors, but the influx of the Americans was on a different scale. They were attracted by the intellectual ferment of Bohemian Paris and the romantic lure of Montparnasse.

Outstanding in recent years has been the continuation of the time-honoured tradition of erecting great public buildings. Only in Paris could the wave of *Grands Travaux* have been undertaken to give us the Grande Arche of the Défense, the Pyramid of the Louvre, the Orsay Museum, the Opéra-Bastille, the Institute of the Arab World, La Villette, the new Bibliothèque Nationale de France and

The Chaillot Palace, seen from the Eiffel Tower.

the Stade de France.

The character of various districts has altered, too. North African, African and Asian immigration, together with newcomers from Eastern Europe, has given a new flavour of cultural diversity. A Far Eastern atmosphere prevails in Belleville and in the XIIIe arrondessement's Chinatown, while North Africa dominates the Goutte d'Or area, alongside Montmartre.

Paris was always thus; wealth and elegance contrasted with a struggle to survive, established power at odds with the energy of newcomers.

There is a small-scale version of New York's Statue of Liberty, by the Allée des Cygnes.

MUST SEE

The River Seine★★★

The Seine gives Paris, more than any other city of Europe, its form and heart. A trip on a riverboat (*bateau-mouche*), starting from the Eiffel Tower, the Pont de l'Alma or the Pont Neuf, not only passes a large number of the finest buildings, but also provides a valuable understanding of the city's layout.

Notre-Dame Cathedral★★★
(Cathédrale Notre-Dame)

The great cathedral of Paris was built between 1163 and 1345. From the towers there are superb views.

Coloured light streams through the stained glass windows of Sainte-Chapelle – breathtaking!

Sainte-Chapelle★★★

This was the private chapel of Louis IX. It is a marvel of the Gothic style, light and radiant with wonderful stained glass.

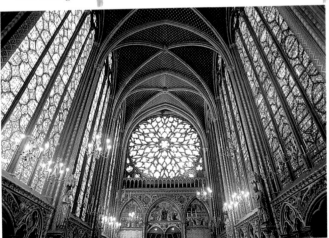

The Louvre★★★
Here one the world's largest collections of European art, from the Middle Ages to 1850, as well as Middle Eastern, Classical and Egyptian works, can be seen and it is worth devoting most of a day to visit it if you can.

Orsay Museum★★★ (Musée d'Orsay)
This was built within the obsolete frame of the old Gare d'Orsay (railway station) to house the nation's collection of 19C and early 20C art, including works by the Impressionists.

The Catholic church of Sacré-Coeur was built at the end of the 19C.

Place des Vosges★★★
Dating from 1609 when it was called the Place Royale, this square cannot be equalled for harmony and grandeur.

Georges-Pompidou Centre★★★
This is one of the city's most startling buildings, as well as being the home of the National Museum of Modern Art.

The Invalides★★★ (Hôtel des Invalides)
This masterpiece of 17C architecture is one of the finest classical monuments in Paris. Napoleon's tomb lies under the royal Dome.

Arc de Triomphe★★★ and the Champs-Élysées★★★
Known to those who have never even visited Paris. It is impossible to leave the city without strolling along the famous avenue or paying homage at the flame of remembrance which burns under the Arch, on the Tomb of the Unknown Soldier.

Eiffel Tower★★★ (Tour Eiffel)
One of the best-known structures in the world, with superb views of the city.

Sacré-Coeur Basilica★★

Standing on the summit of Montmartre,
Sacré-Coeur offers a panorama of Paris and
draws the visitor into the spirit of 19C artistic
creativity that epitomizes the city.

THE ISLANDS AND THE QUAYS★★★
Start: métro Cité Finish: métro St-Michel

Right at the heart of Paris, set like jewels in the waters of the River Seine, are the Ile de la Cité and Ile St-Louis.

Ile de la Cité★★★

This is the historical centre of Paris and in the Middle Ages the island was crowded with buildings, most of which were destroyed when Haussmann undertook the rebuilding of Paris for Napoleon III in the mid-19C. The money ran out before he could complete the transformation, however, and a few old houses survive along Rue Chanoinesse in the north-eastern quarter of the island.

The massive bulk of **Notre-Dame Cathedral★★★** dominates the Place du Parvis, the square facing the west front, but it is

The imposing exterior and entrance to Notre-Dame.

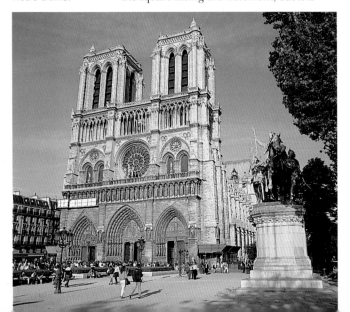

It is worth the climb up the towers of Notre-Dame, not only for the views but to get a closer look at the famous gargoyles.

below ground that the story begins. Under the square, reached by stairs at the western end, the ruins of the Roman town can be seen in the **Archaeological Crypt★** (Crypte Archéologique). Up above, as you approach the cathedral, look for the brass marker set into the pavement. It indicates *Point Zéro*, the place from which all distances from Paris are measured. Before entering the cathedral, climb the towers (buy an entry ticket that includes them) to the **Gallery of Fabulous Beasts** (Galerie des Chimères), or Gargoyles. From here there are wonderful **views★★★** over the city.

Back on the ground, admire the magnificent façade, adorned with statues formerly brightly painted and set in gilded niches, before marvelling at the interior of this Gothic masterpiece. Remember that, before Victor Hugo's novel *The Hunchback of Notre Dame*, with its grotesque character Quasimodo, revived national interest, the building had been sold to a demolition man! The restoration of the decayed cathedral was entrusted to Viollet-le-Duc who, though much criticized by later commentators, recreated the medieval splendour with remarkable success.

The Conciergerie is magical when lit up at night.

Detail from the portal of Sainte-Chapelle.

Within the bulk of the **Law Courts★** (Palais de Justice), the spire of **Sainte-Chapelle★★★** soars. Pray for sunshine and bring your binoculars. Built for St Louis (Louis IX) as a shrine for the Crown of Thorns, this is incontestably the loveliest religious building in Paris. In the nave the lofty walls seem scarcely adequate to support the abundance of superb stained glass.

The western end of the island, reached by the **Quai des Orfèvres** where Inspector

Maigret's real-life equivalents occupy no 36, is linked to the banks of the river by the **Pont Neuf★**, now the oldest bridge in Paris. The pedlars and rogues that once thronged the sidewalks are portrayed in its stonework. The bridge was inaugurated by King Henri IV in 1605 and his statue stands above the little park named after him, the **Vert-Galant Square★**. To the east is the quiet **Place Dauphine★** with its intimate restaurants.

The north-western side of the island is dominated by the **Conciergerie★★**, the 14C fortress-palace of Philip the Fair, boasting Paris's oldest clock. Later, it became death row for over 2 500 victims of the guillotine, including Marie-Antoinette and Robespierre. To cheer yourself up, visit the **Flower Market** in the Place Louis Lépine!

Before crossing to the Ile St-Louis, seek out the eastern tip of the Ile de la Cité. Steps lead down to the austere and moving **memorial** to the victims of Nazi deportations to the death camps.

Ile St-Louis★★

Old façades line the bank of the Seine – shadows of the past emitting incredible charm!

This was developed as a residential area by uniting two separate islands in the 17C. Here you can stroll and watch the patient fishermen and the passing river boats. The great houses, the *hôtels*, face the river. The **Hôtel de Lauzun**, on the Quai d'Anjou, is where the poet Baudelaire had an apartment in the 1850s. It evokes the richness of aristocratic living in its richly decorated interior (not open to the public).

Shops line the central street and this is a good place to buy bread, cheese and wine for a picnic, or seek a light lunch. Ice-cream fit for the gods is sold at no 31, *Berthillon*.

The Quays

Across the river from Ile St-Louis to the
north, on the right bank, the **Hôtel de Ville★**
(the Town Hall) stands in 19C neo-
Renaissance splendour. It was built in the
same style to replace the building destroyed

The Hôtel de Ville, rebuilt in 1874, houses the city's government offices.

Paris at its best stands proudly on display to visitors taking in her sights from the Pont des Arts.

during the revolution of the Commune, in 1871. The square in front of it was formerly called the Place de Grève, the foreshore was where boatmen gathered seeking employment, and where such criminals as Ravaillac, Henri IV's assassin, met grisly deaths.

Further west another square, the **Place du Châtelet**, has taken the place of the huge fortification that guarded the approach to the Ile de la Cité. Two theatres by Davioud face across the square, the **Théâtre Musical de Paris** and the **Théâtre de la Ville**, the latter once owned by Sarah Bernhardt.

The **Quai de la Mégisserie** used to be the centre of the tanning trade, but now supplies gardeners with their plants and animal lovers with their pets. The riverside walls are topped with the stalls of the *bouquinistes*, the second-hand booksellers.

It is worth walking westwards to the **Pont des Arts** to cross the river. This all-iron pedestrian bridge is an ideal viewpoint to rest awhile before admiring the **Institute of France★★** (Institut de France), home of the French Academy (Académie Française), on the south bank. This was the site of the **Hôtel de Nesle**. From its tower a great chain was hung across the river to the Louvre to defend against water-borne attack when this was the western bastion of the city.

East, on the Quai de Conti, the **Hôtel des Monnaies★**, the former Mint, houses a museum of money of interest. The **Quai des Grands-Augustins** has its share of *bouquinistes*, and the walk on eastwards gives you fine views of the islands, and the opportunity to obtain refreshment and a sit-down before continuing on your exploration of the city.

THE LEFT BANK

Start: métro Sully Morland
Finish: métro Solférino or RER Musée d'Orsay

The left bank of the Seine, south of the islands, was the centre of Roman Paris and later, as today, included the university. The **Tournelle** was the fort that shielded this flank of the city, and its name lives on in the bridge and the quay.

Along the river

To the east, overlooking the **Sully Bridge** (Pont de Sully), the vast glass wall of the **Institute of the Arab World★** (Institut du Monde Arabe) faces south, apparently designed to cook those inside the building. Not so; you can spend hours watching the light-sensitive panels adjust to counter the heat, as well as enjoy a fascinating museum and view the river from the roof-top café.

The light sensitive panels of the Institute of the Arab World.

On the river bank is the **Open-air Sculpture Museum** (Musée de Sculpture en Plein Air), inviting a walk amongst the works of art, and alongside are the **Botanical Gardens★★** (Jardin des Plantes) with, on the southern flank, the **National Natural History Institute★★** (*see* p.80). Nearby is the **Mosquée★** where you can enjoy a cup of mint tea – unless you are ready to experience the pleasures of the hammam.

The Latin Quarter★★★

To the west, away from the river, is medieval Paris with its maze of little streets, squares and churches where the **Sorbonne**, the great university, was founded in 1253. Here Latin was the language of scholarship, hence the name of the district. Off the Quai Montebello the little **Church of St-Julien-le-Pauvre★**, as old as the cathedral across the

The Sorbonne was originally a theological college, founded by Robert de Sorbon. This is the Sorbonne Church, erected by Lemercier, which houses the tomb of Cardinal Richelieu.

river, stands in the Square Viviani, off which runs Rue de la Bûcherie with its 13C houses.

Opposite the **Petit Pont**, on the site of the original Roman bridge, the famous English-language bookshop *Shakespeare & Co* sits by a little slice of greenery, together with the last few reasonable cafés. To the left, along Rue du Petit Pont, is the splendid Gothic **Church of St-Séverin★★**. On towards the Boulevard St-Michel fast-food joints and over-priced bars have intruded, but the area is lively with a plethora of Greek restaurants.

Where the Boulevard St-Michel crosses the Boulevard St-Germain you are suddenly faced with monumental Roman remains, the **Baths** (Thermes). Beyond and to the left is another surprise, the **Hôtel de Cluny★**. This 15C *hôtel* now houses a wonderful **Museum of the Middle Ages★★** (Musée du Moyen Âge

The Pantheon, seen from the Luxembourg Gardens.

see p.79). Across the square by Rue St-Jacques you can climb through the modern university to Mons Lutetius, later known as Montagne Sainte-Geneviève, site of the camp of the rebellious Parisii before their defeat by the Romans in 52BC. It is now crowned by the **Pantheon★★** (Panthéon), built by Soufflot in honour of St Geneviève, patron saint of Paris, and devoted to the memory of great citizens of France after the Revolution. Hugo, Rousseau, Voltaire and Zola are among them. The saint herself lies in the nearby **Church of St-Étienne-du-Mont★★** in the company of Pascal and Racine.

Rue Clovis leads to Rue Descartes where a right turn takes you to the **Place de la Contrescarpe★** with its cafés, and beyond to the lively street market and student restaurants in the ancient **Rue Mouffetard★**. A left turn on Rue Descartes brings you to the Place Maubert and the Boulevard St-Germain.

The St-Germain Quarter is full of late-night cafés and bars.

The St-Germain-des-Prés Quarter★★

At the Place St-Germain stands the **Church of St-Germain-des-Prés★★**, last resting place of the philosopher Descartes. The spirits of more recent philosophers and writers, such as Sartre, de Beauvoir and Camus, haunt the **Café de Flore** and the **Deux Magots**; refreshment is costly but worth it for the romantic!

Between the Boulevard St-Germain and the river there are a number of rewarding streets in which to stroll: Rue de l'Ancienne Comédie where the **Café Procope**, haunt of many a literary figure, was established in 1686, Rue de Buci with its street market and Rue St-Benoît, one of the city's jazz-club quarters.

Rue Bonaparte brings you back to the Seine where a left turn on the Quai Malaquais leads to the **Quai Voltaire**. At no 27, on the corner of Rue de Beaune, the writer himself lived until driven away by the noise. He died here only a few weeks after his return from Geneva in 1778. At no 19 is the **Hôtel Voltaire**, a house that has by turns accommodated Baudelaire when working on *Les Fleurs du Mal*, Wagner while composing the *Meistersingers*, and also Oscar Wilde. The remarkable narrow building at no 13 housed Delacroix and Corot, while Ingres, another artist, died next door at no 11.

To the west, on the Quai Anatole France, is the **Palace of the Legion of Honour**, built in 1786 and remodelled by Napoleon in 1804. Opposite is the bulk of the former railway station that is now the **Orsay Museum★★★** (Musée d'Orsay), (*see* p.74).

No 13 Quai Voltaire, once home of Delacroix and Corot.

THE MARAIS★★★

Start: métro St-Paul Finish: métro Hôtel de Ville

The defensive wall built by Philippe Auguste was finished in 1211 and embraced the formerly marshy area to the north of the Ile St-Louis, the Marais. During the next 400 years it became the fashionable quarter of town, with fine *hôtels* to house the rich. By the end of the 19C, however, it had become very run down and more recently narrowly escaped replacement with modern buildings.

Behind and to the east of the **Hôtel de Ville★** is the **Church of St-Gervais-St-Protais★**, named after two Roman soldiers martyred by Nero. The façade is much copied, being a classical arrangement of Doric, Ionic and Corinthian columns. The building guards the approach to Rue François Miron, but closer to the river, at **no 82 Rue de l'Hôtel de Ville**, is the headquarters of the *Compagnons du Devoir* where the work of the craftsmen they nurture can be seen, the practical face of the architectural preservation movement.

Fine Gothic **cellars★** can be seen in the basements of **nos 44-46 Rue François Miron**. These cellars support a wood-framed house typical of the medieval architecture of the district, and a little museum. Further on, the **Maison Européenne de la Photographie** (no 82) has interesting photographic exhibits. The street runs on to the junction of Rue de Rivoli and Rue St-Antoine where the **Church of St-Paul-St-Louis★★**, built by the Jesuits, has Delacroix's *Christ in the Garden of Olives*.

In the gardens behind the church you can see a portion of the old city walls, and the small streets around here still shelter a few workshops of artisans in metal and wood.

Rue St-Antoine leads to the **Place de la Bastille★**, now overlooked by the new opera

The Hôtel de Sully, built in 1625, was bought ten years later by Sully, former minister of Henry IV.

house, but before that, at no 62, stands the beautifully restored **Hôtel de Sully★**, with its striking **courtyard★★**. It is now the head office of the Ancient Monuments and Historic Buildings Commission (la Caisse Nationale des Monuments Historiques et des Sites) and has an excellent information office and bookshop.

Although you can sneak out the back to reach the **Place des Vosges★★★**, the ceremonial entry is from Rue St-Antoine via Rue de Birague and through the King's Pavilion (Pavillon du Roi). The **Place Royale**, as it was originally known – Paris's first square – was built by Henri IV in 1612. A symmetrical poem in faded red brick, it once echoed with the cries of jousting knights. Now it is a fine place to take lunch, either at a restaurant (**Place du Marché Ste-Catherine★**) or in the park with a picnic purchased in the shops of Rue St-Antoine.

After visiting **Victor Hugo's House★** (Maison de Victor Hugo) in the south-eastern corner of the square, leave by the

Street musicians play in the arcades surrounding the lovely Place des Vosges.

opposite corner and **Rue des Francs-Bourgeois★**. Where this crosses Rue de Sévigné the **Hôtel Carnavalet★★** (*see* p.78) and its museum stand, a treasure-house of the history of Paris.

At the next junction the **Hôtel de Lamoignon★**, with a superbly decorated ceiling, houses the Historical Library of the City of Paris. Rue Pavée runs down to the centre of the Jewish quarter on Rue des Rosiers, which has retained its kosher restaurants and ambience.

You cannot miss the sign for the Picasso Museum.

Possibly more deeply moving than the great monuments are the little plaques fixed to the walls in memory of those, young and old, who died at the hands of the Nazis. That fanaticism persists is witnessed by other memorials to more recent atrocities.

Rue Vieille du Temple leads back to Rue des Francs-Bourgeois where a right turn followed by a left turn leads to the the **Cognacq-Jay Museum★★** (Musée Cognacq-Jay), a collection of European art, in Rue Elzévir. Beyond is the **Picasso Museum★★** (Musée Picasso) with the most substantial single collection of the artist's work in existence, now occupying the grand town house (*hôtel*) of a tax-collector (*see* p.77).

No 1 Rue de la Perle is where Libéral Bruant, the architect of the Invalides (*see* p.51), lived. The house, of his own design, is now the **Bricard Museum** of locks and door-knobs. The street leads to Rue Vieille du Temple which passes the **Hôtel de Rohan★★**, with the vigorous **Horses of Apollo★★** by Robert Le Lorrain on the stables, on the way back to Rue des Francs-Bourgeois.

In the other direction no outstanding sights await, but there are numerous little courtyards, as in other streets of the district, with small businesses and factories still making buttons or giving dancing lessons. Don't be afraid to explore! Renoir had his first job here, painting designs for a porcelain manufacturer.

At **no 55 Rue des Francs-Bourgeois is** the Crédit Municipal, a bank which blocks access to **Philippe Augustus's Tower** (Tour de Philippe Auguste), a relic of the medieval fortifications, but you can just see it rising above the gateway at no 57. Opposite, the **Hôtel de Soubise★★**, on the corner of Rue des Archives, is occupied by the **National Archives** and the **Historical Museum of France★** (Musée de l'Histoire de France), with its remarkable 18C decor. Beyond, at no 60 Rue des Archives, is François Mansart's masterpiece, the **Hôtel Guénégaud★★**, now housing the **Museum of Hunting and of Nature★★** (Musée de la Chasse et de la Nature).

As you head south back to the Hôtel de Ville, turn in at no 24 to discover the only medieval cloister in Paris, the **Billets Cloister** (Cloître des Billettes).

BEAUBOURG AND LES HALLES

Start: métro Châtelet Finish: métro Pont Neuf

From the Hôtel de Ville it is a short walk west along Rue de Rivoli to the ornate **St-Jacques Tower**★ (Tour St-Jacques), the last surviving fragment of the 16C **Church of St-Jacques-la-Boucherie** (for this was the butchers' district). From here, pilgrims started their long journey to the shrine of Santiago de Compostela, in northern Spain. In the 17C the scientist Blaise Pascal used

Map of Beaubourg and Les Halles areas.

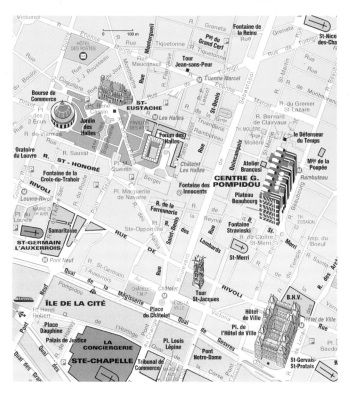

the tower for barometrical experiments, and his rather tatty statue shelters beneath it.

From the other side of the road, Rue St-Martin leads north into the **Beaubourg district**. The **Church of St Merri★**, a corruption of St Mérédic, is a Flamboyant Gothic confection from the 16C, while just round the corner to the right, in the lee of the **Georges-Pompidou Centre**, is the **Stravinsky Fountain★**. With sculptures and brightly coloured mechanical devices that twirl and squirt in the waters; very odd, but fascinating.

The remarkable **Georges-Pompidou**

The fanciful fountain sculptures by Jean Tinguély and Niki de Saint-Phalle, in the Place Igor-Stravinsky.

Centre★★★ gleams above the broad square. Below, the passing crowds pause to watch a juggler or magician entertain, or to observe each other. There are innumerable little cafés and restaurants close by. This multimedia centre offers a wealth of activities. You can watch a film, attend a lecture or preformance, browse through the bookstore or design shop, and consult the open-stack library (levels 2 and 3), while your children have fun in the play area (Galerie des enfants).

The Centre also houses the **National Museum of Modern Art★★★** (Musée

The various street entertainers are always guaranteed an audience outside the Georges-Pompidou Centre.

The modern animated clock, known as Le Défenseur du Temps, *is set on a wall in Rue Bernard-de-Clairvaux.*

National d'Art Moderne; *see* p.73). After visiting the gallery, head up to the terrace on the highest level for the magnificent **views★★★** over the rooftops of Paris. While you're there, take a peek at the restaurant, *Georges*, with its futuristic decor – though you may balk at the prices!

To the north of the Georges-Pompidou Centre lies the residential-commercial complex of the **Quartier de l'Horloge**. The Rue Brantôme (notice the sculpture called *Le Grand Assistant*, by Max Ernst, on the corner) leads to Rue Bernard-de-Clairvaux where you can see an unusual electronic clock known as **Le Défenseur du Temps** (Defender of Time). At noon, 6pm and 10pm this life-size armed figure does battle with three animals symbolising the elements: a dragon (earth), a bird (air) and a crab (water).

From the southern end of the Place Georges-Pompidou a right turn at the Place

The ultra-modern architecture of the Forum des Halles.

E Michelet points you towards **Les Halles** (*see* p.42). On the other side of the Boulevard de Sébastopol, Rue Berger crosses Rue St-Denis, here since the 7C and once the main street of the city.

The further north you go along the ancient thoroughfare, the sleazier it becomes. The square at the junction, Place des Innocents, has a bustling street scene, where you can sit and watch the poseurs or, better, the gyrations of the street-cleaning machines. These little buggies are equipped with long, flexible, trunk-like pipes with which the operators suck up litter.

The Place des Innocents was once a graveyard, and after 2 million skeletons were removed to the Catacombs (*see* p.68) the

Renaissance **Fountain of the Innocents★** (Fontaine des Innocents) was moved here from Rue St-Denis.

The Fountain of the Innocents was designed by Pierre Lescot and carved by Jean Goujon.

Further on, to the right of Rue Berger, is the site of Les Halles, the former wholesale food and produce market of Paris. The first market was erected here in the 12C and by Zola's time had become 'the belly of Paris', with airy iron and glass pavilions. The market has been transferred to the southern suburbs leading to the destruction or relocation of the buildings that had set the style for markets all over France and its eventual replacement with a huge shopping mall – **Forum des Halles★**.

Here, apart from shops, there is the **Holography Museum** and the **Forum des Images**, which is a movie-lover's paradise. There is also a range of cultural and sports amenities.

The large modern sculpture of head and hand by Henri de Miller contrasts with the Gothic exterior of St-Eustache Church.

Across the gardens, the great bulk of **St-Eustache Church★★** looms, and in the Place R. Cassin in front of it a huge stone head and hand attract children. Nearby is a curious sun-dial which channels light along glass-fibre tendrils that light up the appropriate dot on the scale of the hours.

Directly south, by Rue des Prouvaires, Rue du Roule and Rue de la Monnaie, the river lies and, overlooking it, the great department store of **La Samaritaine** in all its *belle époque* glory. If you venture to the roof-top café, refreshment and **views★★** over the Seine will provide a lasting reminder of the beauty of Paris.

THE LOUVRE TO THE ARC DE TRIOMPHE

Start: métro Palais-Royal – Musée du Louvre
Finish: métro Charles de Gaulle – Étoile

The Louvre★★★

There has probably been a fortress of some kind on the site of the **Cour Carrée★★★** of the Louvre since Roman times, but the first incorporation of it into the city was instigated by Philippe Auguste in the 13C, who made it a bastion of his new wall. With the spread of the city to the west the need for it as a military installation ceased, and

Construction of the Louvre Palace.

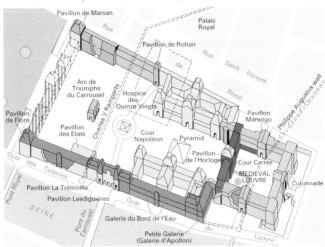

EVOLUTION OF THE LOUVRE PALACE

Built under Philippe Augustus	Added by Louis XIV
Built under François I	Added by Napoleon I
Added by Henri II and Catherine de'Medici	Built under Louis XVIII
Added by Henri IV	Added by Napoleon III
Added by Louis XIII	Added under the Third Republic

----- No longer exists

The Flore and Marsan Pavillions were rebuilt after the fire of 1871.

As you move from courtyard to courtyard, when night falls, the subtle lighting and the luminous glass pyramid, with the cupola of the Institut and the arcades outlined below – truly magical!

from the 16C onwards it was rebuilt and restyled as a royal palace.

Catherine de Médicis added the **Tuileries Palace** to the west and the two grew together until Louis XIV made Versailles his residence in 1678. Various offices and apartments were made within it until, in the mid-19C, a great renovation was started. As a boy, Renoir and his family were forced to move out of their flat to make way for the reforms.

In 1747, a room was set aside to permit students to view parts of the royal art collection, such as the *Mona Lisa* acquired from Leonardo da Vinci by François I. In 1793, the decision was taken to turn it into a national museum, and in 1981, President Mitterand put the 'Grand Louvre' project in

hand, getting rid of the remaining governmental offices and devoting the whole complex to art.

A new entrance was designed by I M Pei to give access to the galleries from an underground entrance hall, entered by a translucent **pyramid★★**. An **inverted pyramid★** complements the original one and provides light to a large shopping arcade, **Le Carrousel du Louvre** (*see* p.101), virtually under the same roof as the Louvre, with display areas, shops, cafés and restaurants.

The Louvre collection is huge, but careful planning before plunging into the galleries is recommended. European art from the Middle Ages to 1900, plus Oriental, Egyptian and classical art, are represented here as nowhere else (*see* p.71).

Tuileries Gardens★ (Jardin des Tuileries)

If you are daunted by the crowds in the Louvre, or just plain tired, go to the **Orangery Museum★★** (Musée de l'Orangerie) at the far end of the Tuileries Gardens on the river side (*see* p.74). The matching pavilion on the other side is the **Jeu de Paume**, formerly a real (indoor) tennis court, which now has temporary exhibitions of contemporary art.

The gardens were laid out by Le Nôtre for the palace that was burned down under the Commune in 1871. Wander here to see the children sail hired boats on the pond and wonder at the modern sculptures (including Rodin, Moore and Giacometti).

To the east, the royal parish **Church of St-Germain-l'Auxerrois★★** displays a medley of architectural styles that witness its long life. From its tower, the bells rang out in 1572 to initiate the Massacre of St-Batholemew in which thousands of Huguenots perished.

Twelve avenues radiate out from the Arc de Triomphe, the grandest being the Champs-Élysées.

The Champs-Élysées★★★

Within the arms of the Louvre stands the **Arc de Triomphe du Carrousel★**, the first of a series of arches. Napoleon built this to celebrate his victories. Beyond, the better known **Arc de Triomphe★★★**, also by Napoleon, looms at the end of the Champs-Élysées in line with **La Grande Arche★★** at **La Défense★★** (*see* p.82).

The **Place de la Concorde★★★**, at the end of the Tuileries Gardens, was built to honour Louis XV. It drew vast crowds during the Reign of Terror, for it was here that the Sanson family (executioners), impeccably clad with a flower in their buttonhole, sped their victims to eternity by means of Dr Guillotine's cunning machine. Its name was changed from 'Révolution' in a spirit of conciliation and the focus changed with the arrival of the Obelisk from Luxor, a gift from the Viceroy of Egypt in 1829. Two fountains inspired by those in St Peter's Square, Rome, provide a decorative touch, with eight statues representing cities. From the central reservation topped by the **Obelisk★** there is a superb **view★★★** of the Champs-Elysées.

The floodlit Place de la Concorde is a romantic square to wander round in the evening, though the traffic can be alarming.

There are bargains for philatelists at the Stamp Market in the Cour Marigny.

To the north are the twin mansions of the **Hôtel de la Marine★★** and the **Hôtel Crillon★★** – the latter overlooked the guillotine, standing near the statue representing Brest, where Louis XVI died.

The Champs-Élysées, with Le Nôtre's tree-planting, designed to enhance the vista from the Tuileries, is now the most famous thoroughfare in the world. Gardens flank the first part, with the **Grand Palais★** and **Petit Palais★**, built for the 1900 World Exhibition, to the left and the **Théâtre Marigny** to the right. At weekends the **Stamp Market** (Marché aux Timbres) is held in the Cour Marigny.

Turn left at the Rond Point down the Avenue Montaigne to the *haute couture* area, with Yves St-Laurent, Dior and Balmain. At the junction of Rue François 1er there are plaques set into the sidewalk commemorating two of the greatest fashion designers. Turn right here to the Avenue Georges V and back to the Champs-Élysées.

The **Étoile**★★★, the star of roads at the western end of the Champs-Élysées, is now the **Place Charles-de-Gaulle**, but the huge **Arc de Triomphe**★★★ stays the same. Planned in 1806 by Napoleon as a memorial to the warriors of France, it took 30 years to finish. In 1920 it became the shrine of the Unknown Soldier and the flame of remembrance was first lit in 1923. From the top there is yet another unmissable vista.

The opportunity to sit down and take in the sights is welcome at this street café on the Champs-Élysées.

THE INVALIDES TO THE EIFFEL TOWER

Start: métro Invalides Finish: métro Trocadéro or métro Avenue du President Kennedy – Maison de Radio-France

The Dome Church (Église du Dôme) houses the tomb of Napoleon directly under the famous gilded dome.

The Invalides*** (Hôtel des Invalides)

From the right bank, cross the **Alexandre III Bridge**✶✶ and the Esplanade to reach the Invalides, a masterpiece of classical architecture. Built for the 1900 World Fair, the Alexandre III Bridge consists of a single

surbased arch that does not block the view.

The Esplanade is sufficiently long to give ample opportunity to admire the symmetrical layout of the buildings in the Invalides. Beyond the gardens decorated with cannons lies the **Main Courtyard★** (Cour d'honneur) flanked by the buildings now occupied by the **Army Museum★★★** (*see* p.78).

Louis XIV's reign was marked by wars that were costly in terms of manpower and money. He was the first monarch to take an interest in army veterans. He commissioned the liberal-minded Bruant to set up the Invalides which was opened in 1674. Jules

The elaborately decorated lamp-posts on the Pont Alexandre III, with the exuberant Grand Palais in the background.

Hardouin-Mansart continued the work after Bruant's early death. The **Dome Church★★★** (Église du Dôme), Louis XIV's private chapel, was built to the conventional layout used by the new architect. Until it was turned into a mausoleum for military heroes by Napoleon, there used to be a door between the church and the more austere 'Soldier's Chapel', **St-Louis des Invalides★**. Napoleon's remains were returned here from St Helena in 1840, and he is now buried in six coffins encased in a red porphyry tomb. Other leading figures buried in the Dome Church include Joseph and Jérôme Bonaparte and the field marshals Foch and Lyautey.

Leaving the Église du Dôme on your right, the **Jardin de l'Intendant** contains the moving memorial to the victims of terrorism, a sculpted fountain *Parole portée*, by Nicolas Alquin, on the Boulevard de La Tour Maubourg.

Other Sights

Next to the Invalides to the east, on Rue de Varenne, is the **Hôtel Biron★★**, where Auguste Rodin lived from 1908 until his death. It houses the **Rodin Museum★★** (Museé Rodin – *see* p.77).

Walking west of the Invalides by the Avenue de Tourville, and enjoying a lesser-known view of the Dôme, brings you to the **French Military Academy★★** (École Militaire), the officer's academy founded in Louis XV's time. Shortly after its opening it became the Higher Officers' School and enrolled, amongst others, a young man called Napoleon Bonaparte who graduated as a lieutenant in the artillery.

The great parade ground, the **Champ-de-**

Mars*, stretches down from the academy to the River Seine. Now pleasure gardens, they have been used for various exhibitions and celebrations, notably the Exhibition of 1889 when they were covered with great iron-framed pavilions, and when the Eiffel Tower was erected by the riverside. Montgolfier's hot-air balloon took off from here in 1783.

The Eiffel Tower*** (Tour Eiffel)

For people throughout the world the Eiffel Tower is the symbol of Paris, yet when first built it had to endure the insults of the arbiters of aesthetics, who were only too pleased to think that it was soon to be torn down, and the gloomy forecasts of the financial pundits that it would lose money. Now the exuberant confidence of its shape delights, and as for the money, of the 7½ million francs it cost to build, 6 million were recouped in the first year.

Although 318m (1 043ft) high, it weighs less than the cylinder of air that contains it. Some 300 men took 26 months to make it, and used 2½ million rivets in the process.

During the high season there are long queues for the elevators, but it is well worth the wait. You can climb the stairs to the first two levels. On the first there is a short film in the **Cinémax**, on the second an expensive restaurant (with access by private lift) and on the third, a superb **view*****.

Other Sights

In front of the Eiffel Tower, the Seine is crossed by the **Pont d'Iéna**, named after Napoleon's victory at Jena and threatened with destruction by Blücher after the British and Prussian success at Waterloo. Boats depart for river trips from here.

Paris seen from on high: from the Eiffel Tower, the terraces of La Samaritaine and Beaubourg, the towers of Notre-Dame or the dome of Sacré Coeur – different angles, different heights...but the spectacle is always magnificent!

The fountain-bedecked **Trocadero Gardens**★★★ (Jardins) clothe the flank of the little hill on which Catherine de Médicis built her out-of-town country house. The site is now occupied by the **Chaillot Palace**★★ (Palais de Chaillot), constructed for the 1937 Paris Exhibition and the home of four museums. Partial damage by fire resulted in the closure (until 2003) of the **Museum of**

The Eiffel Tower, seen from across the Seine.

French Monuments★★ (Musée des Monuments Français – *see* p.80) and of the **Henri Langlois Film Museum** (Musée du cinéma Henri Langlois). The latter will be moving to the future Maison du Cinéma in the former American Center, near Bercy, but films will still be shown at the **Film Library** (Cinémathèque). You can always visit the **Maritime Museum★★** (Musée de la Marine) and the **Museum of Mankind★★** (Musée de l'Homme) or go to the Théâtre National de Chaillot, under the **terrace★★★** (temporarily closed for renovation). Le Totem café-restaurant, on the right wing of the Chaillot Palace, has magnificent **views★★★** of Paris.

Downstream, the double-decked bridge, the **Pont de Bir-Hakeim**, carries cars below and the *métro* above. From here, the **Allée des Cygnes** runs down the centre of the river beyond the **Pont de Grenelle**, where a miniature of New York's Statue of Liberty stands, given to Paris by the American colony in 1885.

The statue of Joan of Arc in the Place des Pyramides.

THE PALAIS-ROYAL TO THE OPÉRA

Start: métro Palais Royal – Musée du Louvre
Finish: métro Palais Royal – Musée du Louvre or
métro Pyramides

The Palais Cardinal was built for Louis XIII's minister, Cardinal Richelieu, and later became an additional residence for the royal family when it was renamed the **Palais-Royal★★**. Beyond the main court, filled with the pillars of Buren's candy-stick sculpture, the great courtyard garden is surrounded by delightful colonnades behind which are exclusive galleries and shops.

Enclosed by golden gates, surrounded by arcades supporting elegant façades, the Jardin du Palais Royal is a haven of peace in the heart of the city...

Across Place du Palais-Royal and to the right, **Rue de Rivoli★** runs beside the Louvre to the **Place des Pyramides** with its statue of Joan of Arc. The **Museum of Decorative Arts★★** (Musée des Arts Décoratifs) at no 107, and the **Fashion and Textile Museum★** (Musée de la Mode et du Textile) next door, with on its third floor a new section dedicated to the **Musée de la Publicité**, are well worth a visit. Going on up Rue des Pyramides, a left turn on **Rue St-Honoré★** takes you to the **Church of St-Roch★**, notable mainly as the resting place of the great garden designer Le Nôtre and of writers Corneille and Diderot.

Further on to the right, the wide space of the **Place Vendôme★★** opens before you; though much admired as an early 18C masterpiece, you may find it a souless place, well suited to the hard-nosed bankers and jewellers who took up residence here.

A warmer welcome (at a price) is found at the **Ritz Hotel** (admirers of Hemmingway will recall the author of *The Old Man and the Sea*, while having a drink at the bar which bears his name). In the centre of the

The famous Maxim's, on Rue Royale.

square, the column recording Napoleon's victories is modelled on Trajan's Column in Rome.

From Place Vendôme take Rue St-Honoré to Rue Royale, sporting at no 3 the famous façade of **Maxim's** and its annex, **Minim's**. Nearby, Rue du Faubourg-St-Honoré boasts a wealth of big-name fashion boutiques and art galleries with elegant window displays.

At the top of the Rue Royale stands the classical façade of the **Madeleine**★★, as the church dedicated to St Mary Magdalene is popularly known. It faces the colonnaded **Palais-Bourbon**★ on the other side of Place de la Concorde. Around the back, in the Place de la Madeleine, are **Fauchon** and **Hédiard**, emporiums that every food fanatic should visit.

For more modest shoppers, the Boulevard Haussman, to the north, offers **Printemps** and **Galeries Lafayette**, from which you can turn south to the **Opéra**★★, also to be found by going along the Boulevard de la Madeleine and the Boulevard des Capucines.

The **Opéra Garnier** is a testament to the aspirations of the 19C. The **Grand Staircase** and **Grand Foyer** are a riot of materials and decoration, as is the auditorium itself with the curious contrasting ceilings by Chagall.

Join the regulars at the sidewalk terrace of the **Café de la Paix** on the northwest corner of the **Place de l'Opéra★★**, but save some money for shopping in the exclusive shops on the **Avenue de l'Opéra★**. Or head down the Boulevard des Italiens to Boulevard Montmartre and let your imagination run wild at the **Grévin Museum★** (Musée Grévin), with its true-to-life wax figures.

The **Passage Jouffroy** next door and the **Passage des Panoramas** across from it are

With a huge perfume hall, Printemps is one of the oldest department stores in Paris.

both worth exploring. To reach the **Passage Choiseul**, take Rue Vivienne alongside the **Stock Exchange** (La Bourse), then Rue St-Augustin.

Food and book-lovers might want to go on to **Drouant**, the restaurant on the Place Gaillon where the Prix Goncourt literary prize has been awarded since 1914.

Going on towards the **Place des Victoires★** on Rue des Petits Champs, swing through the glass-roofed **Galerie Vivienne**, with its elegant boutiques, then continue down Rue Croix des Petits Champs to **Galerie Véro-Dodat**, where the beautiful shops are matched only by the splendid decor. Heading down Rue de Richelieu, stop by the **Comédie-Française**, and if you're in luck you may also get tickets to see a classical play. Finally, don't miss the delightful Palais-Royal metro station, adorned with beads, created by artist Jean-Michel Othoniel.

The Opéra, begun in 1848, was not completed until 1875.

MONTMARTRE***

Start: métro Place de Clichy or métro Blanche
Finish: métro Place de Clichy

From **Place Blanche**, with the hill of Montmartre rising above, the first romantic vision of this area in the north of the city is confirmed, for across the street is the windmill-adorned façade of the **Moulin-Rouge**. No longer the casual venue of Lautrec's time, it offers a slick show for out-of-town crowds – great fun, all the same.

The Boulevard de Clichy to the east leads to the **Place Pigalle**, a quarter recovering slowly from extreme sleaziness. The café that occupied 9 Place Pigalle, the **Nouvelle Athènes**, was the haunt of Renoir, Manet, Pissarro and Cézanne and provided Degas, who lived at no 6 Boulevard de Clichy, with the setting for the painting known as the *Absinthe Drinkers*. Lautrec had a studio at no 5 Avenue Frochot (closed to non-residents).

Map of Montmartre.

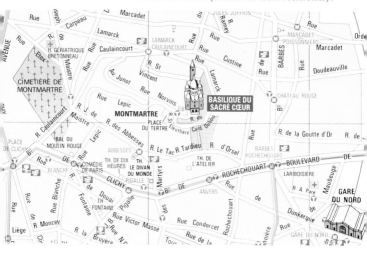

Turning left up Rue des Martyrs, past no 75 which was the **Divan Japonais** (now a fashionable nightspot, *Divan du Monde*), for which Lautrec made a poster, and left into Rue des Abbesses, brings you to the **square★** of the same name in which the *métro* entrance stands. It is one of only a few of the originals in the Art Nouveau style of Guimard to survive intact.

Rue des Abbesses runs on to Rue Lepic, where local people shop, and where Vincent

The many narrow cobbled streets and steep steps give Montmartre its characteristic village feel.

A Toulouse-Lautrec poster of Aristide Bruant from 1893.

and Théo Van Gogh lived at no 54, but you can reach the **Place Émile-Goudeau★** either by the Passage des Abbesses or by cutting through to Rue des Trois Frères.

At no 13 **Place Émile Goudeau★ Le Bateau-Lavoir** used to stand. The wooden building creaked and swayed like the moored barges on the Seine that were used by washerwomen, according to the poets and artists who frequented it. Here **Cubism** was born. Picasso and Braque lived and worked here, and today's artists use the rebuilt studios and apartments.

Rue d'Orchampt cuts through to the long curve of Rue Lepic at the new site of the **Radet mill**, but up to the left in its original

The Place du Tertre has always been a popular meeting place, and is now a busy tourist spot.

position is the **Moulin de la Galette**, a flour mill that was turned into a dance hall when modern methods replaced it. In 1814 it was defended against the Cossacks by the miller whose corpse was crucified upon the sails as revenge for his defiance. A happier memory of it is as a place of entertainment, shown in a painting by Renoir in the Orsay Museum and, less well known, one by Picasso.

Heading to the right up Rue Lepic brings you to the junction of Rue des Saules and Rue Norvins, which leads to the **Place du Tertre★★**. Here you could be forgiven for thinking you have stepped into a painting by Utrillo. Busy streets, but the crowds are part of the delight, and the artists in the square are an integral part of the decor. Some of their works will provide amusing souvenirs.

Beyond the Place du Tertre and **St Peter's Church★** (Église St-Pierre) towers the **Sacré-Coeur★★**. The basilica was built in a fervour of religious penitence after the Franco-Prussian war and is best enjoyed from a distance or as a superb **look-out point★★**.

Off Rue du Mont Cenis at no 12 Rue Cortot is the **Museum of Old Montmartre** (Musée du Vieux Montmartre) in an old house where Renoir, Suzanne Valadon, Utrillo and Dufy had studios. Exhibitions of contemporary art and evocations of the past are to be seen here. Next to it, on Rue des Saules, is the only surviving vineyard in Paris and, at the next crossroads, the cabaret theatre **Lapin Agile**.

Over the wall facing the theatre is the **St-Vincent Cemetery** (Cimetière St-Vincent), but to get in you have to work your way around it clockwise. Utrillo's grave is here.

More richly populated and decorative is the **Montmartre Cemetery** (Cimetière de Montmartre), some way to the west by Rue Caulaincourt. The detailed map displayed there will allow you to discover the graves of Degas, Nijinsky and François Truffaut, among many others. A short walk takes you to the **Place Clichy** and the cafés immortalized by Pierre Bonnard.

One of the numerous street artists at work in the Place du Tertre.

MONTPARNASSE AND LUXEMBOURG PALACE AND GARDENS

Start: métro Montparnasse – Bienvenüe
Finish: métro St Germain des Prés

Montparnasse★★

Picasso, like so many avant-garde artists, poets and writers, moved from Montmartre to Montparnasse on the other side of the city in 1912, and for nearly 30 years this became the intellectual and artistic capital of the world. Sadly, little remains due to

Map of Montparnasse and Luxembourg areas.

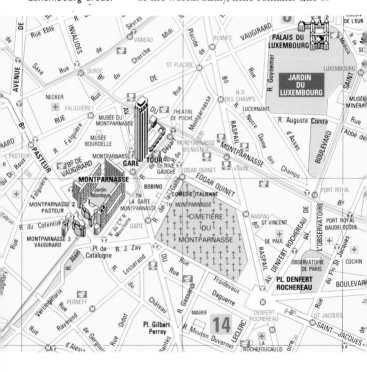

development in the 1970s. However, the intrusive skyscraper, the **Montparnasse Tower★★** (Tour Montparnasse) is now an accepted part of the skyline. From the top, there is a breathtaking **panoramic view★★★** of the city.

To the west are two museums, the **Postal Museum★** (Musée de la Poste) for philatelists and the **Bourdelle Museum★★** (Musée Bourdelle) in the street also named after this pupil of Rodin; some of his works can be seen here. If you're looking for somewhere to relax, walk around the railway station (Gare Montparnasse) and enjoy a moment in the **Atlantic Garden★** (Jardin de l'Atlantique), built above the tracks. Two figures from the Resistance, Field Marshal Leclerc and Jean Moulin, are remembered in two museums located next to the station.

From Boulevard Edgar-Quinet, take a glimpse at Rue de la Gaîté, once lined with cafés, dance halls and other places of entertainment. There are now a few high-quality theatres, including the Comédie Italienne (no 17), Théâtre de la Gaîté-Montparnasse (no 26) and Théâtre Montparnasse (no 31).

The main entrance to the **Montparnasse cemetery** is back on the boulevard, where there is a plan of the burials. Sartre and de Beauvoir lie here, with Jean Seberg, Citroën Baudelaire, César Frank, Maupassant and Serge Gainsbourg. *The Kiss* by Constantin Brancusi (and Brancusi himself) is also here.

Nearby is the Carrefour Vavin, a junction overlooked by a statue of Balzac by Rodin. Cafés here, made famous by leading intellectuals of the interwar years, include the **Dôme**, **Rotonde**, **Coupole**, and **Sélect**. The **Closerie des Lilas**, a favourite haunt of Hemingway, among others, is further east at 171 Boulevard du Montparnasse. From the crossroads, follow Boulevard Raspail south, passing the **Fondation Cartier** (designed by Jean Nouvel) which houses temporary exhibitions of modern art. From Place Denfert-Rochereau, you can visit the **Catacombs★**, an underground ossuary. On the square, there are two pavilions by Ledoux – the city's toll gates until 1870.

Luxembourg Palace and Gardens★★
Return to Boulevard Montparnasse, then go along Avenue de l'Observatoire. The Observatory **fountain★** was designed by

The Luxembourg Gardens are atmospheric, even in winter.

Davioud and is famous for the four areas of the world carved by Carpeaux. Enjoy the fine view to the Luxembourg, through the trees. The **Palais du Luxembourg★★** to the north was built for Marie de Médicis in the Italian style. The buildings now house the Senate, the upper house of the French parliament. As you enter the gardens through the less formal part, take care not to interfere with the games of *boules*, or collide with biking children, for this is a public garden enjoyed by the local citizens.

On the eastern flank of the palace is the Italianate **Medici Fountain★** (Fontaine de Médicis), while the **Orangery** is on the west. To the north, the great bulk of the **Church of St-Sulpice★★** rises. Many hands were involved in the design of this huge church. The façade has little stylistic connection with the rest, and was never finished as planned. Within are **murals★** by Delacroix (1st chapel on the right).

Going north once more towards the **St-Germain-des-Prés Quarter**, there are narrow streets with numerous little shops, including some high-fashion establishments, before finding the cafés of Boulevard St-Germain.

A popular spot for playing a game of boules is the Luxembourg Gardens.

MAJOR MUSEUMS

One of the best ways to economize and save time when visiting the museums of Paris is to obtain a **Museum and Monuments Pass** (Carte Musées et Monuments), which also applies to certain public monuments such as the Arc de Triomphe. The participating museums let you in with no further charge, and an added bonus is that you go straight to the entrance without queuing! The regulations change from time to time, however, so be sure to pick up the current brochure when you buy your pass. It lists the museums and monuments to which the pass applies, with brief details of each place, including opening times.

Most municipal museums are closed on Mondays and national museums on Tuesdays and some bank holidays.

The pass can be bought either at one of the museums, at major *métro* stations or at the National Tourist Bureau, 127 Avenue des Champs-Élysées. You can get a pass for 1, 3 or 5 days, valid from the day it is first used (so you can buy one in advance). The actual saving on entry fees depends on where you visit, but roughly speaking a 1-day pass saves money on the fourth place visited, a 3-day pass on the eighth place and a 5-day pass on the eleventh museum entered. For special exhibitions, a supplementary payment may be required.

On the third weekend of September an Open Day for Historical Monuments gives free entry to many major attractions, as well as entry to many places open to the public on that weekend alone. This facility is much used by locals and the museums can get quite busy.

Art Museums

Guimet Museum★★ (Musée Guimet)
6 Place d'Iéna, *métro* Iéna
This museum of Asian arts, including Khmer, Indonesian, Tibetan, Chinese and Japanes works, is one of the most important in the world.

Jacquemart-André Museum★★ (Musée Jacquemart-André) 158 Boulevard Haussmann, *métro* St Philippe-du-Roule
Formerly a private collection of French 18C paintings and furniture, 17C Dutch paintings and Renaissance art, including Uccello's *St George and the Dragon*, in a 19C mansion.

The Louvre Museum★★★ (Card-holders enter by the Passage Richelieu from Rue de Rivoli. Otherwise enter by the Pyramid in the Cour Napoleon, *métro* Palais Royal). To avoid queueing, use the Minitel (3615

The Richelieu Wing in the Louvre.

*Michelangelo's
Dying Slave, in the
Louvre.*

Louvre; www.louvre.fr) or ☎ 01 40 20 51 51
to obtain a ticket that is valid for any day of
the week.

You could spend a month here, so take
the time to pick up a plan of the museum
from the information area and work out
your route. The Oriental and ancient
European and Egyptian collections are
huge; they include the *Seated Scribe, Vénus de
Milo* and the *Winged Victory of Samothrace.*
Leonardo's *Mona Lisa* (known in France as
La Joconde) and Michelangelo's *Dying Slave*
are among the Renaissance works here. The
French artists represented include Georges

The old railway station has provided a splendid home for the Orsay Museum.

building-for-old to house the most magnificent collection of art from the years 1848 to 1914, including the Impressionists.

On entering, pick up a plan of the museum as the signposting is poor. Works are shown in roughly chronological order.

The ground floor leads through the periods of Classicism and Romanticism (Ingres and Delacroix) to the Barbizon school (Corot, Millet, Courbet) and then to early Impressionism (Manet, Monet). You then go up to the top level to see the astonishing wealth of Impressionist and post-Impressionist work, including such familiar friends as Renoir's *le Moulin de la Galette* and *The Swing*, Degas's *Blue Dancers*, Van Gogh's *A Room at Arles* and Cézanne's *L'Estaque*. The riches continue – Seurat's *The Circus*, Toulouse-Lautrec's *Jane Avril Dancing*, Gauguin's *Tahitian Women* and Bonnard's *Women in a Garden*.

Refresh yourself with a turn on the terrace beyond the café before descending to the middle level and the Art Nouveau section.

The Picasso Museum, housed in a beautiful restored mansion, has a fine collection of the artist's works.

Don't miss the International section either, which shows how this essentially French movement has been interpreted elsewhere. Less familiar to many is the school of the Nabis.

Museum of Modern Art of the City of Paris★★ (Musée d'Art moderne de la Ville de Paris) Palais de Tokyo, 11 Avenue du Président-Wilson, *métro* Iéna
The municipal art collection is often missed by visitors. Housed in a building constructed for the 1937 Exhibition, it has good coverage of the Cubists, the Fauves and the Paris School. Dufy's huge **La Fée Électricité★** is a contender for the largest painting in the world. Contemporary artists are represented too, and temporary exhibitions held.

Picasso Museum★★ (Musée Picasso) Hôtel Salé, 5 Rue de Thorigny, *métro* St-Paul
The finest collection of Picasso's work is displayed here. From the Blue Period through his exploration of Cubism to the joyous and humorous works of his later life, including ceramics and sculpture, the amazing creativity of the artist can be appreciated. There are also works by other artists (Braque, Cézanne, etc) from Picasso's personal collection.

Rodin Museum★★ (Musée Rodin) Hôtel Biron, 77 Rue de Varenne, *métro* Varenne
It is particularly interesting to visit the place in which the sculptor worked and lived. It is even more satisfying to be able to enjoy his creations in the setting of a beautiful garden, as well as in the house itself. *The Kiss, The Burghers of Calais, The Gates of Hell* and *The Thinker* are here, as are studies for his controversial statue of Balzac (*see* p.67).

Gustave Moreau Museum★★ (Musée Gustave Moreau) 14 Rue de La Rochefoucauld, *métro* St-Georges
In the home and studio of this artist, a leading figure in the Symbolist Movement, are more than 6 000 works ranging from sketch pads to huge oil paintings.

OTHER MUSEUMS
Army Museum★★★ (Musée de l'Armée)
Hôtel des Invalides, *métro* Invalides or Varenne
The military past of France is covered well, but the museum also traces warfare from prehistoric times to the present day. The cinema shows film of the First World War from 2.15pm and of the Second from 4.15pm.

Carnavalet Museum★★ (Musée Carnavalet)
23 Rue de Sévigné, *métro* St-Paul or Chemin-Vert
This museum of the history of the city of Paris is housed, in part, in the Hôtel Sévigné, residence of the famous 17C writer Madame de Sévigné. Paintings, furniture and decorative items illustrate past lifestyles, with models of the city at various stages of its growth. The history of the Revolution and the Reign of Terror is well covered. The orangery at the Hôtel Le Peletier houses pieces from Paris' beginnings to Antiquity, including dugout canoes found under the Bercy wine warehouses.

City of Science and Industry★★★ (Cité des Sciences et de l'Industrie) – La Villette Park
30 Av Corentin-Cariou, *métro* Porte-de-la-Villette
An amazing complex of buildings erected on the site of the former meat market and slaughterhouses, this is much more than a single museum; it is a new city park with space to play, have a picnic or take a stroll.

The Museum of the Middle Ages has a fine collection of works of art and decorative objects.

The thematically arranged main museum is possibly the most exciting science museum in Europe. The **Géode**★★★ is an unusual spherical-shaped cinema for which, as for the **Children's City**, card-holders must pay extra.

Music Museum★ **(Musée de la Musique)**
Avenue Jean-Jaurès, *métro* Porte-de-Pantin
A sound and vision walk, through both old and contemporary instruments. A must!

Museum of the Middle Ages★★ (Musée du Moyen Âge) 6 Place Paul Painlevé, *métro* St-Michel or Cluny la Sorbonne
Within the beautiful residence of the Abbots of Cluny is a superb collection of medieval masterpieces. The highlight is the famed **The Lady and the Unicorn★★★** tapestries. The Gallo-Roman **Baths★** (Thermes) house ancient sculptures, with stained glass, carvings and illuminated books.

Museum of Mankind★★ (Musée de l'Homme) Palais de Chaillot, Place du Trocadéro, *métro* Trocadéro
Covers the history of the human race with exhibits from all over the world, and includes an especially interesting music section.

Maritime Museum★★ (Musée de la Marine) Palais de Chaillot, Place du Trocadéro, *métro* Trocadéro
The largest maritime museum in the world, with models, charts, paintings and details of Napoleon's plans to invade England.

Museum of French Monuments★★ (Musée des Monuments Français) Palais de Chaillot, Place du Trocadéro, *métro* Trocadéro
The copies gathered here show the decorative sculptures, paintings and stained glass that adorn the country's greatest buildings (closed for renovation).

National Natural History Institute★★ (Muséum National d'Histoire naturelle) 57 Rue Buffon, *métro* Gare d'Austerlitz
The **Botanic Gardens★★** have as their centre-piece the **Grande Galerie de l'Évolution★★★**. Other sections, including a maze and tropical greenhouse, are spread around the gardens.

FURTHER AFIELD

La Défense★★

It can be seen from afar, but the vast scale of La Grande Arche can only be appreciated when you get close to it.

On the western edge of Paris you will see, looking from the Tuileries or from the Arc de Triomphe, another arch, apparently plain, white and square. Take the RER or *métro* out there and you will discover just how massive it is: some 92m (300ft) high!

La Grande Arche★★ is the focus of a modern business district, **La Défense★★**, a phalanx of skyscrapers providing essential space for big business, previously strangled by the over-crowding of central Paris. They stand around the wide square with modern sculptures and computer-controlled fountains to humanize the space. Apart from La Grande Arche (the trip to the top in the outside lifts provides a panoramic view of the capital), the **Musée de l'Automobile★★** and the **Dôme Imax**, in La Défense business district, also attract many visitors.

The Basilica of St Denis★★★

To the north of Paris, the town of St Denis, at the end of the no 13 métro line (St-Denis-Basilique) was, in the 19C, covered by rather

The vaulted interior of the Basilica of St Denis.

unattractive industrial estates. Only the famous **Basilica★★★** attracted visitors up until the building of the **Stade de France★** (where the 1998 Football World Cup took place) revived the area.

The Basilica is where Gothic architecture began. Under the direction of Abbot Suger in the 12C, what was already the burial place of the kings of France was rebuilt in a new style. Pointed arches and rose windows first amazed and delighted onlookers here. The arrangement of the façade was revolutionary and widely followed, with its three portals and decorative sculpture. The choir has the first ribbed vaulting, and the precedents for the rose windows and thematic stained glass of Chartres Cathedral are here also.

Flea Market, St Ouen★

One of three such markets, but the largest and most famous, St Ouen is reached (note carefully!) from the *métro* Porte de Clignancourt. Head north, along the Avenue de la Porte de Clignancourt and under the *périphérique* to reach the area

The open-air flea market near the Porte de Clignancourt has many a bargain awaiting discovery!

The Géode, in La Villette Park, is a huge silver mirrored dome with a hemispherical cinema screen inside.

outside the city gates where the traders in junk were able to ply their wares. Left on Rue des Rosiers, you'll find the **Marché Biron★** and an information point where you can get a guide to the maze (*Guide des Puces*). The range of market stalls is great, from junk stalls to specialist stores offering high-priced antiques (open Saturday to Monday).

La Villette Park★

Mentioned here because you can travel by boat (*see* also p.78). From the centre of the city you can depart from either the Quai Anatole-France near the Orsay Museum, or from the Arsenal Marina near the Place de la Bastille (as services are infrequent check

times with Canauxrama ☎ 01 42 39 15 00, or
Paris Canal ☎ 01 42 40 96 97).

Père-Lachaise Cemetery★

Reached by the *métro* station of the same
name, this vast cemetery has become a place
of pilgrimage for people of diverse interests.
Political historians revere the scene of the
execution of the last rebels of the Commune
at the **Federalists' Wall** in the south-eastern
corner, while fans of the Doors rock group
weep over the grave of Jim Morrison.

Medieval romantics seek out Abélard and
Héloïse, music lovers Chopin, Bizet and
perhaps Édith Piaf, literary types Molière, La
Fontaine, Alfred de Musset, Gertrude Stein,
Proust and Oscar Wilde, and art lovers
Géricault, Delacroix, David and Modigliani.
Film lovers can pay homage to Simone
Signoret and Yves Montand.

*Detail of Oscar
Wilde's tomb by
Jacob Epstein. Wilde
is just one of the
many famous laid
to rest in the Père-
Lachaise Cemetery.*

OUT OF TOWN

Disneyland Paris★★★
Marne-la-Vallée. 32km (20 miles) east of Paris,
on autoroute A4. RER line A4.
Although it got off to a troubled start, the
huge theme park appears to be establishing
a character of its own. The classic favourites,
Mickey Mouse and the other Disney
characters, have pride of place but new
attractions are being added and economy-
minded visitors catered for.

Five principal 'magic lands' are featured:
Main Street USA, a small American town at
the turn of the century; Frontierland, a
glimpse of the old Wild West; Adventure-
land, ranging from the mysteries of the East
to Caribbean pirates; Fantasyland, centred
on the Sleeping Beauty's castle and, the
latest of all, Discoveryland, where Space
Mountain offers intergalactic travel.

Six hotels serve the complex, each
representing a particular region of the USA
and ranging in level from the luxury to the
economy. Also, there is golf, swimming,
cycling, a pony-club, tennis and, in winter,
ice-skating, as well as extensive shopping and
evening entertainment facilities.

Fontainebleau★★★ *By train from the Gare de*
Lyon to Fontainebleau-Avon and then bus to the
château, or by car via the A6 and N7.
Basically the 16C palace built for François I,
subsequent monarchs added new courtyards
and wings so that Napoleon described it as
'the house of the centuries'. Quite as
interesting as the lavish interiors are the
gardens★, themselves the outcome of
evolutionary growth rather than a single
overall design.

The Renaissance palace of Fontainebleau.

Enjoy a walk in the **forest★★★** (*some areas are off-limits due to the 1999 storms*). While you are in the area, you can also visit the village of **Barbizon★★** and the **Château de Courances★★**.

It is difficult to do justice to the Palace of Versailles and the gardens in a single visit.

Versailles★★★ *By RER train, line C5 to Versailles Rive-Gauche or SNCF train from the Gare St Lazare or from Montparnasse.*

Louis XIV's minister, Nicolas Fouquet, started something when he invited his king to the unveiling of his palace at **Vaux-le-Vicomte**★★★ (also worth visiting). He ended up in gaol and the king ordered his architect, Louis Le Vau, and his garden designer, André Le Nôtre, to turn the hunting lodge used by his father, Louis XIII, into a luxurious palace at Versailles.

Although full of tourists and long queues, this 17C palace has to be seen. More a theatrical set than a home, a full tour of the palace and grounds takes a couple of days. If time is limited, start with the first floor, which has the most splendid apartments. After the devastating storm in 1999, the project to restore the French **gardens**★★★ to their original state was begun earlier than planned. But have a walk through the park anyway to get to the Grand and Petit Trianon and the Hameau. If you can, catch the **Fêtes de Nuit** (on certain Saturday evenings, June- Sept).

Museum card-holders should enter gate A2 (Chapel Courtyard), and must pay extra for the King's Chamber and Lecture Tour.

Vincennes★★ *métro Château de Vincennes.*
Château de Vincennes is almost within the city. Set in a large wooded park with a zoo, a lake and the **Parc floral de Paris**★★, it is a lovely contrast to city sights. The château has a medieval keep, the **Donjon**★★, contrasting with Le Vau's 17C palace and buildings.

The **Museum of African and Oceanian Art**★ (Musée des Arts d'Afrique et d'Océanie) is on the western side of the **Bois de Vincennes** (*métro* Porte Dorée), offering a return route to the city without retracing your steps.

ENJOYING YOUR VISIT

Getting Around

Visitors' Paris is not a huge area, and walking is the best way to see the unexpected along with the great monuments. To get from one place to another, public transport is excellent. The national railways (SNCF), the urban expresses (RER), the metropolitan underground railway (*métro*) and the bus service combine to offer a service that will meet almost every need.

The city is divided into zones to define ticket validity, zones 1 to 3 covering everywhere suggested in this book except the Out of Town locations, which are in zones 4 and 5, as are the major airports.

Tickets

The key to untroubled, casual use of the transport system is the purchase of a *Paris Visite* ticket. These are available for either 2, 3 or 5 day periods, and for either zone 1 to 3 or zone 1 to 5 use. A leaflet giving exact details of how and where to use the card, and of various special discount offers, comes with the card.

For longer periods of stay in Paris, weekly and monthly tickets are available. You get an identification card (carte orange – the size of a credit card) and a ticket that will activate automatic barriers. Don't lose either of them, and remember to pick up the ticket when it has passed through the automatic barrier mechanism. You do not need to punch the ticket on buses.

Métro

Métro lines are identified by colour codes on the map and a number at the terminal stations at either end. The direction in which the train is going is indicated by the name of the terminus, for example, 'Ligne 12, Porte de la Chapelle'. The RER lines have letters, A, B, etc, and their branches, as they approach the outskirts of town, each has an additional number. RER trains are fast and stop at fewer intermediate stations than the *métro*; check the departure board beneath the luminous panels, to be sure it stops where you want to go. *Métro* tickets give access to RER trains in the Paris area.

Buses

Do not be afraid of the buses! Although the numbered routes may appear hard to understand, the *Paris Visite* leaflet suggests a few routes of special interest to the visitor. The buses have a route map inside, marked with the stops which are announced or are clearly signed on the bus stops. Just show your *Paris Visite* card when you get on; ordinary bus tickets are cancelled by pushing them in the machine, but the *Paris Visite* card is not. The **Batobus** is a waterborne bus service along the Seine.

Panoramic buses make it easy

The red métro sign is easy to spot.

for you to discover the city without getting tired. **Opentour** provides a circular route which includes 21 stops (tickets can be bought on the buses, at hotels and at the Tourist Office), whilst **Paribus** has nine stops (buy your ticket on the bus). In both cases, the tour lasts around 2 hours and you can get on and off as you wish with the same ticket, which lasts two days running.

Driving in Paris

As in any major city, traffic in Paris is always heavy and driving conditions can be difficult, especially at peak times. If you are nevertheless ready to face the traffic jams, difficulties with parking, and the sometimes agressive and, to say the least, impatient style of driving inherent to the Parisians, read the practical information at the end of this guide book (**Driving**) before taking to the wheel of your car.

WEATHER

Like other northern European cities, Paris has fairly even rainfall throughout the year, about 50mm (2in) per month, with spring months often being rather showery, and August the wettest month. An umbrella is always useful!

The temperature ranges from about 5°C (40°F) in December and January to 24°C (76°F) between June and August. April, May, September and October are pleasantly moderate.

Daylight hours are long in the summer, when the evening extends to 9 or 10pm.

This is a maritime climate, usually without extreme conditions, but the weather is changeable so a fine morning can give way to a showery afternoon, and rain at breakfast time can yield to clear skies by lunchtime.

CALENDAR OF EVENTS

There is always something happening in Paris! To find out all the details, ask for the *Paris Sélection* brochure from the Tourist Office (127 Avenue des Champs-Elysées). It gives an indication of the main events being staged each month in the city. The full programme of shows is published every Wednesday in *Pariscope* and *Officiel des Spectacles*, on sale in newspaper kiosks.

A few outstanding events:
Six Nations Tournament, Stade de

France. February to March. International rugby.

Salon International de l'Agriculture Parc des Expositions de Paris, Porte de Versailles. Early March.

Paris Marathon Departure from the Champs-Elysées. Arrival Avenue Foch. One Sunday at the end of April or beginning of May.

Final of French Football League Cup (Coupe de France) Stade de France. May.

Internationaux de France de Tennis Roland Garros Stadium, Avenue de la Porte d'Auteuil (*metro*: Porte d'Auteuil). French open tennis championships. End of May, beginning of June.

Festival Chopin Bagatelle, Bois de Boulogne. Mid-June to mid-July. Piano recitals in the Orangery at Bagatelle.

Fête de la Musique Throughout the city. 21 June. Numerous concerts (often free) ranging from classical to rock.

14 July (bank holiday). A national event. In Paris, there is an impressive military parade down the Champs-Elysées. Fireworks and dances all over the place!

Festival d'été Various locations. 15 July to 15 August.

Festival Musique en l'Île Music festival in various churches: Sainte-Chapelle, St-Louis-en-l'Ile, Saint-Germain-des-Prés. Mid-July to early September. Classical music concerts, oratorios, chamber music.

Tour de France This famous cycle race finishes on the Champs-Elysées at the end of July.

Festival d'Automne Various locations throughout the city (Théâtre du Châtelet, Théâtre de la Ville, L'Odéon-Théâtre de l'Europe). Mid-September to mid-December. Drama, music and dance.

Mondial de l'Automobile (Motor show, even-numbered years) and **Salon International de la moto** (Motorbike show, odd-numbered years). Parc des Expositions de Paris, Porte de Versailles. Early October.

Festival de Jazz Various locations throughout Paris. End of October.

Horse racing Grand Prix de l'Arc de Triomphe, Longchamp. First Sunday in October. Grand Prix d'Automne, Auteuil. Early November.

Foire internationale d'Art contemporain (FIAC) October. One of the largest international art fairs in Europe.

Festival d'Art Sacré de la Ville de Paris In churches and cultural venues throughout Paris. End of November to mid-December.

Paris by night

A trip through **Paris by night** is unforgettable! Some of the streets and avenues such as the **Champs-Elysées**, **Avenue Montaigne**, **Rue Royale** or **Boulevard Haussmann** are a dazzlingly magical sight, especially at Christmas. Look out for the **banks of the Seine**, the **Louvre** (the **Cour Carrée** is an even more prestigious sight by night), the **Cour Napoléon** and the **Pei Pyramid**, the **Palais-Royal** and the arcades around the Comédie Française, **Place de la Concorde**, the **Champs-Elysées** up to the Arc de Triomphe, the **Esplanade du Palais de Chaillot** and the **Eiffel Tower**, the **Invalides**, the **St-Germain-des-Prés** district, the **Institut de France** and, of course, **Notre-Dame** and the **Ile St-Louis**.

ACCOMMODATION

From a palatial grand hotel to a more modest affair, there is something to suit everybody's taste and pocket in Paris (prices, alas often high, are indicated in brackets and correspond to the minimum for a single room and the maximum for a double room). For a romantic break, here are a few suggestions for some hotels steeped in charm, though rather expensive (137-381 € for a double room):

Pavillon de la Reine 28 pce des Vosges (3e) ☎ 01 40 29 19 19
Lutèce 65 rue St-Louis-en-l'Ile (4e) ☎ 01 43 26 23 52
Deux Iles 59 rue St-Louis-en-l'Ile (4e) ☎ 01 43 26 13 35, fax 01 43 29 60 25
Les Rives de Notre Dame 15 Quai St Michel (5e) ☎ 01 43 54 81 16, fax 01 43 26 27 09
Relais Christine 3 rue Christine (6e) ☎ 01 40 51 60 80, fax 01 40 51 60 81

Relais St Germain 9 carrefour de l'Odéon (6e) ☎ 01 44 27 07 97, fax 01 46 33 45 30
Relais Médicis 23 rue Racine (6e) ☎ 01 43 26 00 60, fax 01 40 46 83 39
La Villa 29 rue Jacob (6e) ☎ 01 43 26 60 00
Duc de Saint Simon 14 rue St-Simon (7e) ☎ 01 44 39 20 20, fax 01 45 48 68 25

For more modest budgets, there are plenty of **less luxurious** but less expensive hotels (Max. price 91.5 € for a double room):

Familia 11 rue des Écoles (5e) ☎ 01 43 54 55 27, fax 01 43 29 61 77
Pierre Nicole 39 rue P. Nicole (5e) ☎ 01 43 54 76 86, fax 01 43 54 22 45
Empereur 2 rue Chevert (7e) ☎ 01 45 55 88 02, fax 01 45 51 88 54
Muguet 11 rue Chevert (7e) ☎ 01 47 05 05 93, fax 01 45 50 25 37
Champ de Mars 7 rue du Champ de Mars (7e) ☎ 01 45 51 52 30, fax 01 45 51 64 36
Nord et Est 49 rue Malte (11e) ☎ 01 47 00 71 70 fax 01 43 57 51 16
Grand Hôtel Prieuré 20 rue Grand Prieuré (11e) ☎ 01 47 00 74 14, fax 01 49 23 06 64
Acropole 199 Bd Brune (14e) ☎ 01 45 39 64 17, fax 01 45 42 18 21
Châtillon H. 11 square Châtillon (14e) ☎ 01 45 42 31 17, fax 01 45 42 72 09

Favart 5 rue Marivaux (2e) ☎ 01 42 97 59 83, fax 01 40 15 95 58

Delhy's 22 rue de l'Hirondelle (6e) ☎ 01 43 26 58 25

New Orient 16 rue de Constantinople (8e) ☎ 01 45 22 21 64, fax 01 42 93 83 23

Istria 29 rue Campagne Première (14e) ☎ 01 43 20 91 82, fax 01 43 22 48 45

Delambre 35 rue Delambre (14e) ☎ 01 43 20 66 31, fax 01 45 38 91 76

Hameau de Passy 48 rue de Passy (16e) ☎ 01 42 88 47 55, fax 01 42 30 83 72

For information on youth hostels, *see* p.111.

TAKING A STROLL

As soon as there is a ray of sunshine, it is tempting to take a stroll through the city streets or stop for a drink at a pavement café. Give in to temptation! You will be amply rewarded by the sheer delight of all that you discover.

Try and find the 135 bronze medallions dotting the cobble-stones of Paris, a homage to astronomer François Arago (1786-1835).

On the fronts of apartment blocks, read the **plaques** in memory of the famous and less famous who have lived and loved this city.

Have a rest in one of the new **parks** – the Parc André Citroën and its colourful gardens, the Jardin Atlantique laid out over the concrete precinct that covers the

railway lines at Montparnasse Station, the Parc de Bercy which stands on the site of the erstwhile wine market, or the Parc de Belleville with its many terraces and waterfalls.

Wander through the labyrinth of **arcades** leading onto the main boulevards, idling away some time in the second-hand book shops or stores specialising in antique toys.

At some street corners, you may be confronted by **trompe-l'oeil paintings** on the walls – people peeping out of a window on the Piazza Beaubourg, or a fireman on his ladder in rue de Ménilmontant (20e). In other places you will find **sculptures** by César (rue du Four), Zadkine (Beaubourg), or Picasso in St-Germain-des-Prés. Take a look at the **African market** in the 18e or the Chinese markets in the 13e or Belleville. You can perhaps end your stroll in one of the bistros where Parisians meet and set the world to rights.

FOOD AND DRINK

France is famous for its gourmet cuisine and its capital, Paris, has some of the country's very best restaurants. If you are having a slightly longer break, dining in one of these great restaurants is also a way of appreciating French traditions and heritage. Paris is a cosmopolitan city offering a whole range of exotic flavours in the numerous restaurants providing dishes from all over the world.

To help you pick out the

Street musicians add colour and vitality to the festivities.

restaurant you want, the *Michelin Red Guide France* includes a selection of restaurants in its 'In and Around Paris' section. The restaurants are classified per *arrondissement*, amenities and quality. From famous addresses which are well worth the trip in their own right (but where the prices are high) to smaller establishments with reasonable prices, the cuisine is of the same high quality. There are other restaurants serving regional or foreign specialities. In fact, you are sure to find one that will suit your taste and your pocket (*for a selection of addresses, see below*).

The information brochures available from the Tourist Office or from your hotel also provide detailed lists and a range of information, including prices.

Meals

Breakfast can be taken either *sur le zinc* (at the bar counter) in true Parisian style or at a table in the one of the many pavement cafés. It can consist of black coffee, tea or a *petit/grand crème* (large or small white coffee) with a croissant, bread and butter or a *petit déjeuner complet* consisting of fruit juice, croissant, bread, butter, jam and a hot drink.

The area around the Bastille has the largest number of *brasseries* providing an almost round-the-clock service.

To relax after a day of sightseeing or a show, there are restaurants and cafés all over Paris, even inside some of the museums (Louvre, Musée d'Orsay, Palais de Chaillot, Centre George-Pompidou, Institut du Monde Arabe etc.), monuments (Eiffel Tower) or certain theatres (Lucernaire, 6e; Théâtre du Rond-Point, 8e; Théâtre de la Colline, 20e) and cinemas (Le Latina, 13e; L'Entrepôt, 14e).

In some of the Parisian parks (Montsouris, Buttes-Chaumont, Palais-Royal, Tuileries, Luxembourg, Bois de Boulogne), there are restaurants with tables set outside. They are often delightful, if expensive, places to have lunch or dinner in the summer. Simpler, but equally enjoyable, is the cafeteria in the Rodin Museum or in the Café Véry in the Tuileries Garden. On a warm day, why not buy the ingredients for a picnic and sit in a park or near the Seine, on the banks of the Ile Saint-Louis or in the Square du Vert-Galant?

If you are determined to find some really exotic food, head for the pedestrian streets around the Church of St-Séverin, at the end of boulevard St-Michel, in rue Mouffetard behind the Pantheon or in the Bastille area.

For dinner, having worked up an appetite with a good day's sightseeing in the city, choose a restaurant. If you have somewhere precise in mind, it is best to book in advance and arrive on time. If you have not yet decided where to go, study the menus displayed outside. The prices are clearly indicated and there may be fixed or special-price menus which are usually good value for money.

Since the so-called 'Evin Law' was passed, most restaurants are supposed to have separate areas for *fumeurs* (smokers) and *non-fumeurs* (non-smokers), although some have opted for a single, non-smoking area.

By law, restaurants are obliged to indicate prices inclusive of service charge but it is polite to leave a few coins, or up to 5% of the cost of the meal if you are satisfied with the service.

Restaurants, cafés, bistros and brasseries

The exact meaning of each of these terms is not strictly adhered to but the following hold more or less true:

Restaurants serve copious meals with three courses or more. It therefore takes time to eat in a restaurant. For a less formal meal (and usually a more convivial atmosphere), choose a **bistro**. The cuisine is traditional and it is acceptable to have only one course.

A few addresses:

Benoît 20 rue St-Martin (4e) ☎ 01 42 72 25 76. Attractive decor, very good food.

Petit Bofinger 6 rue de la Bastille (4e) ☎ 01 42 72 05 23. 1950s decor. Good value for money.

Grizzli 7 rue St-Martin (4e) ☎ 01 48 87 77 56. A bistro dating from the days of the old market (*Les Halles*).

Allard rue St-André-des-Arts (6e) ☎ 01 43 26 48 23. A traditional bistro.

Bistrot St-Honoré 10 rue Gomboust (1e) ☎ 01 42 61 77 78. A pleasant family-run bistro.

P'tit Troquet 28 rue de l'Exposition (7e) ☎ 01 47 05 80 39. A delightful bistro popular with locals.

La Fontaine de Mars 129 rue St-Dominique (7e) ☎ 01 47 05 46 44. A traditional 1930s bistro. Known for its extensive use of fresh produce.

Chardenoux 1 rue Jules Vallès (11e) ☎ 01 43 71 49 52. Beautiful turn-of-the-century decor.

À la Grille Montorgeuil 50 rue Montorgeuil (2e) Typical bistro cuisine in what was, in the heyday of Les Halles, a butchery. Superb counter and vaulted cellar.

Perraudin 157 rue Saint-Jacques (5e) ☎ 01 46 33 15 75. Good bistro

Enjoying a drink at a café is a central part of any visit to Paris.

fare, with tasty dishes reminiscent of the cuisine of the past.

Régalade 49 avenue J-Moulin (14e) ☎ 01 45 45 68 58. A very popular local bistro.

Bistrot du Dôme 1 rue Delambre (14e) ☎ 01 43 35 32 00. Seafood bistro.

A **café** serves mainly drinks but it will also provide snacks and light meals. In some cases, a café may actually serve full meals like a restaurant. In this case, the menu will be displayed outside.

New trails...

Next to well known spots, new trendy places appear and disappear following the fashion of the time. This movement, which has already been around for a few years in the **Marais** (rue Vieille-du-Temple and nearby), then in **La Bastille**, rue de Lappe (*L'An vert du décor*, *Tapas Nocturne*), rue de Charonne (*La Fontaine*, *Chez Paul*), rue St-Sabin (*Les machines*, *Bali Bar* and *Café de l'Industrie*), rue Fbg St-Antoine (*Sanz Sans*, *Barrio Latino*) has continued further north to the foot of Ménilmontant, rue Oberkampf (*Cithea*, *Café Charbon*, *Mecano Bar*, *Blue Billiard...*).

To the east of Paris, things are also moving, especially in the 20th *arrondissement*, with *La Flèche d'Or* (rue de Bagnolet). Along the **Saint-Martin canal**, on a level with the Quai de Valmy, *Chez Prune*, *La Marine* and *Atmosphère* are trying to created an ambience, whilst near

the Seine in the **Bercy village**, the *Vinea Café* (in the same style as the *Viaduc Café*, set under the Viaduc des Arts), *Nicolas* and the *Compagnie des Crêpes* welcome film buffs from the UGC Ciné-Cité. On the other bank, Quai François Mauriac, the DJs from *Batofar* entertain insomniacs until all hours.

Brasseries originated in Alsace and were linked to beer and the food that goes with it. They have now become traditional haunts, often popular with the famous and the jet set and often serving very high-quality meals. The decor is sometimes 'turn-of-the-century'. *Brasseries* serve all types of dishes and their opening times are much longer than the opening hours of conventional restaurants. Some serve meals almost round-the-clock.

The ubiquitous baguettes – part of French life.

The best-known include:

Au Pied de Cochon 6 rue Coquillière (1e) ☎ 01 40 13 77 00. Open round the clock.

Gallopin 40 rue Notre-Dame-des-Victoires (2e) ☎ 01 42 36 45 38. A fine *brasserie* with authentic late 19C decor.

Bofinger 5 rue de la Bastille (4e) ☎ 01 42 72 87 82. Superb turn-of-the-century decor.

Bouillon Racine 3 rue Racine (6e) ☎ 01 44 32 15 60. Belgian food in Art Nouveau decor.

La Fermette Marbeuf 1900 5 rue Marbeuf (8e) ☎ 01 53 23 08 00. 1900 decor, with ceramics, stained-glass windows and a beautiful period piece – a glass dome.

Mollard 115 rue St-Lazare (8e) ☎ 01 43 87 50 22. Known for its listed restaurant, the work of Edouard Niermans, it is spacious with beautiful mosaics and Sarreguemines earthenware. Good brasserie cuisine.

Au petit Riche 25 rue Le Peletier (9e) ☎ 01 47 70 68 68. Late 19C interior.

Flo 7 cour des Petites Ecuries (10e) ☎ 01 47 70 13 59. 1900s decor.

Julien 16 ru du Faubourg St-Denis (10e) ☎ 01 47 70 12 06. Decor Belle Époque.

Train bleu Gare de Lyon (12e) ☎ 01 43 43 09 06. 1900s decor. Frescoes of the trip from Paris to the Mediterranean coast.

La Coupole 102 bd du Montparnasse (14e) ☎ 01 43 20 14 20. A vast restaurant with 1920s decor. Noisy but worth a visit for the atmosphere.

Other *brasseries* deserve a mention for the view they offer of some of the city's most prestigious sights and buildings:

Café Marly, Cour Napoléon (1e);

Choosing what to eat can be a serious business.

ENJOYING YOUR VISIT

Brasserie de l'Ile St-Louis, 55 quai Bourbon (4e); *Le Vauban*, 7 place Vauban (7e); *Chez Francis*, 7 place de l'Alma (8e).

Wine bars can be either come-as-you-are or highly-sophisticated. They are user-friendly venues, favoured by Parisians with a knowledge and love of good wine. Served by the glass or in a pitcher, the wine can be accompanied by cheese or a plate of *charcuterie* (sausage, ham etc.).

The following list of convivial addresses is, of course, far from comprehensive:
Les Pipos 2 rue Polytechnique (5e); *Au Sauvignon*, corner of rue de Sts-Pères and rue de Sèvres (6e); *Sancerre* 22 avenue Rapp (7e); *L'Ecluse* 15 place de la Madeleine (8e); 64 rue François Ier (8e); 13 rue de la Roquette (11e) and 1 rue d'Armaillé (17e); *Jacques Mélac* 42 rue Léon Frot (11e); *L'Opportun* 62/64 boulevard Edgar Quinet (14e); *Le Sancerre* 35 rue des Abbesses (18e); *Bistrot-Cave des Envierges* 11 rue des Envierges (20e).

Give yourself a **gastronomic treat** (after all, you are in Paris!). There are plenty of addresses to choose from. Among the city's leading restaurants are:
L'Ambroisie 9 place des Vosges (4e) ☎ 01 42 78 51 45.
L'Arpège 84 rue de Varenne (7e) ☎ 01 45 51 47 33.
Lucas Carton 9 pl de la Madeleine (8e) ☎ 01 44 95 15 01.
Alain Ducasse 59 avenue R. Poincaré (16e) ☎ 01 47 27 12 27.

SHOPPING

Paris may be world-famous for fashion and *haute couture* houses, but not far from the prestigious windows of the luxury boutiques and large department stores are other places which are particularly popular with Parisians.

The **Marais** boasts a number of leading names in its old streets, and has shops a-plenty. In and around the **Forum des Halles** and near **place des Victoires**, there is an equally vast choice.

St-Germain-des-Prés is famous for its antique shops, art galleries, fabric shops and antique furniture in the picturesque streets running between boulevard St-Germain and the Seine. Explore the labyrinth of streets between St-Germain-des-Prés and St-Sulpice if you are looking for books and gifts.

In addition to **Fauchon**, **Hédiard** or **Pétrossian** (8e), all famous as the places to shop for grand occasions, gourmet visitors will find baker's shops (Poilâne, 6e and 15e), ice-cream parlours (Berthillon, 4e) and wonderful cake shops (Carton, rue de Buci, 6e; Peltier, rue de Sèvres, 7e; Dalloyau, rue du Faubourg-St-Honoré, 8e; Carette, pl du Trocadéro, 16e). Another sight not to be missed is the **Grande Epicerie de Paris**, beyond the Bon Marché department store in rue de Sèvres (7e).

Flower markets (place Louis-Lépine, place de la Madeleine, place des Ternes) and the **St-Ouen flea market** are also worth a visit. There are further flea markets in Montreuil and Vanves. The **Carreau du Temple** is famous for its leather clothing while the Parc Georges-Brassens is the setting for an **antique and second-hand book market** at weekends. Each district of the city has its own open-air market and French equivalent of the car boot sale.

Paris also has a number of large department stores that should be part of any visit to the capital. On boulevard Haussmann, near the Auber RER station and *métro* station Havre-Caumartin are **Printemps**, **Galeries Lafayette**, and **Marks & Spencer's**. **La Samaritaine** is at Pont-Neuf; there is a wonderful view from its terrace. Shopping malls such as **Forum des Halles**, **Maine-Montparnasse**, **Beaugrenelle**, **Trois Quartiers**, **Atrium du Palais** (a shopping mall underneath the Palais des Congrès at Porte Maillot) and **Carrousel du Louvre** are also worth visiting.

In rue de Sèvres on the left bank is **Le Bon Marché**, the prototype for later department stores.

After the pleasures of strolling through the city streets and doing a spot of shopping, why not have a rest in a friendly **tea room** such as: *Angelina* 226 rue de Rivoli (1e). *Cador* 2 rue de l'Amiral Coligny (1e).

The inverted pyramid in the underground shopping complex, the Carrousel du Louvre.

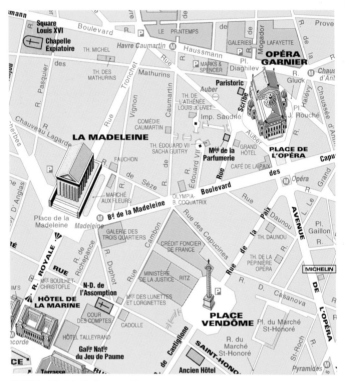

Map showing Boulevard Haussman with its famous department stores

Café Marly Palais du Louvre 93 rue de Rivoli (1e).

The decor is modern and austere but it is a good place to relax after visiting the museum.

A priori thé 35 galerie Vivienne (2e).

Pandora 24 passage Choiseul (2e). This tea room, like the previous one, is located in one of the district's numerous arcades.

L'apparrament Café 18 rue Coutures St-Gervais (3e). One of the most fashionable tea rooms at the present time. Do try any of the board games available to customers.

La charlotte-en-l'île 24 rue St-Louis-en-l'Ile (4e).

Mariage Frères 13 rue des Grands-Augustins (6e). Offers 400 varieties of tea.

La Samaritaine department store.

La Mosquée 39 rue Geoffroy-St-Hilaire (5e). Exotic decor in which to savour mint tea and oriental pastries.

Chez les filles 64 rue du Cherche-midi (6e) A cosy, quiet atmosphere.

Le Lutetia 23 rue de Sèvres (6e). In the prestigious surroundings of the hotel of the same name.

Christian Constant 26 rue du Bac (6e). Remember to taste the chocolates.

Ladurée 16 rue Royale (8e) and 75 av des Champs-Elysées (8e). A very chic tea room where the most elegant Parisiennes savour the famous home-made macaroons.

Tea Folies 6 place G. Toudouze (9e). Near the Gustave Moreau Museum.

Carette 4 place du Trocadéro (16e). Chic and expensive.

L'été en pente douce 23 rue Muller (18e). On the Montmartre hillside.

Le Gastelier 1 bis rue tardieu (18e). View of the Sacré-Coeur.

Le Crillon 10 Place de la Concorde (1er). Undoubtedly a must as a tea room of class, being part of a prestigious hotel chain.

Jean-Paul Hévin 231 rue St-Honoré (1er). Tasty pastries.

Toraya 10 rue St-Florentin (1er). The ambassador for Japanese tea.

L'Artisan des saveurs 72 rue de

Cherche-Midi (6e). An address for hungry tourists, combining sweet and savoury with tea served as it should be.

Tea Tattered Pages 24 rue Mayet (6e). A peaceful back room in and English secondhand bookshop.

Tch'a, La Maison de Thé rue du Pont-de-Lodi (6e). The art of tea-drinking in a timeless setting.

ENTERTAINMENT AND NIGHTLIFE

There are so many different ways of having an evening out in Paris!

To find out what is on each week in the city, consult *L'Officiel des Spectacles* and *Pariscope* (on sale in newspaper kiosks), *Paris Sélection* (a free monthly magazine published by the Paris Tourist Board) or the *Figaroscope*, a Wednesday supplement to the daily *Figaro* newspaper. You can also consult the Minitel, 3615 CAPITALE.

Tickets for shows can be purchased in any agency in the city centre. **Alpha-FNAC** has an agency in the Forum des Halles, on floor 3. There are other agencies throughout the city.

Reviews and Shows

The most spectacular reviews are to be seen at the **Moulin-Rouge** (82 boulevard de Clichy, 18e), and the **Lido** (116 avenue des Champs-Elysées, 8e). Rows of leggy dancers, magicians, singers and other turns entertain the diners and members of the audience who come only to see the show. At the **Crazy-Horse** (12 avenue George V, 8e), superb dancers provide a dazzling display of talent with unusual choreography. Undoubtedly one of the finest of all the Paris reviews and is, at the very least, a 'once in a lifetime' experience.

Cabarets

The traditional cabaret, with witty songs and satirical monologues, still exists. The **Caveau de la Bolée** (25 rue de l'Hirondelle, 6e), the **Lapin Agile** (22 rue des Saules, 18e), and the **Don Camillo** (10 rue des Saints-Pères, 7e), are particularly good examples.

Café-theatres such as the **Café de la Gare** (41 rue du Temple, 4e), **Au Bec Fin** (6 rue Thérèse, 1e) and the **Café d'Edgar** (58 boulevard Edgar-Quinet, 14e) provide an opportunity to enjoy Parisian wit and new talents.

Music in Paris

Paris is a major centre of music, in auditoria large and small, churches, museums, and even river barges.

Then there are the traditional concert halls (Pleyel, Théâtre des Champs-Elysées etc.) and cultural institutions such as the newly-renovated Olympia. In fact, Paris has concert halls that are as diverse in programming as they are outstanding in decor. The **Opéra-Bastille** plays host to major international creations throughout the season. The **Opéra Garnier** specialises in classical ballet and

The Moulin-Rouge offers colourful and lively entertainment.

modern dance.

The **Cité de la Musique** stages contemporary and ethnic works, in a building full of curves designed by Portzamparc. The **Zenith** and **Bercy** sports hall are used for large popular music concerts.

Every year, in January, the City Council launches a promotional event called 'Book one seat and bring a friend'. A second seat is included, free of charge, for anybody booking a seat for a concert in one of the 54 halls and religious buildings involved in this operation which lasts for a fortnight. More than 300 concerts of classical and contemporary music and jazz are staged over this period.

Music in Paris can also mean the accordeonist playing in a local market, the notes of a saxophone on the banks of the Seine, a song being performed in the métro, South American music on the Piazza de Beaubourg, or the sharp sound of the *qin* in the Chinese district.

Jazz

Paris remains one of Europe's leading centres for jazz. Clubs, caverns and night clubs provide evening entertainment in St-Germain-des-Prés, Les Halles and Montparnasse. Major American artistes make Paris a priority venue on any European tour.

The success of clubs such as **New Morning** (7-9 rue des Petites-Ecuries, 10e, *métro* Château-d'Eau),

ENJOYING YOUR VISIT

Latitudes Jazz Club and **Montana** (rue St-Benoît, 6e, *métro* St-Germain-des-Prés), the **Duc des Lombards** (42 rue des Lombards, 1e), the **Petit Journal Montparnasse** (13 rue du Commandant-Mouchotte, 14e), or the **Petit Journal St-Michel** (71 boulevard St-Michel, 5e), the **Caveau de la Huchette** (5 rue de la Huchette, 5e) is fully deserved.

At the end of July, there are jazz evenings in the inner courtyard of a superb mansion in the Marais district, the Hôtel d'Albret (31 rue des Francs-Bourgeois, 4e). Jazz is also performed at La Villette.

Sacred music

A Festival of Sacred Art is held at the end of November in many Parisian churches, chapels and synagogues. This provides a means of (re-)discovering a wide range of prestigious venues by listening to organ concerts, medieval music, the famous unaccompanied singers of Corsica or Liguria and numerous other choirs. Information: ☎ 01 53 45 17 00.

Cinemas

Paris has over 350 cinemas, most of them in the Opéra district and along the main boulevards, from the Odéon to the Latin Quarter, in Montparnasse, and on the Champs-Elysées. Every week, they show more than 300 films, many of them foreign films in the original language with French sub-titles (indicated in programmes as 'V.O.').

The cinemas renew their programme every Wednesday. Some of them offer reduced rates in the mornings and afternoons, or on Mondays or Wednesdays.

Those who enjoy watching giant screens will appreciate cinemas such as the **Grand Ecran Grenelle** (15e), the **Grand Rex** (2e), the **Grand Ecran Italie** (13e), the **MK2 Quai-de-Seine** (19e) or the 14 screens of the **Aquaboulevard** (15e).

Most of the cinemas specialising in experimental films are to be found in the Latin Quarter (**Accatone, Racine, Studio des Ursulines, Reflet Médicis** and **Reflet Logos**). All of them are well-known to Parisian filmgoers.

Theatres

The Paris area has more than 100 theatres, in districts around the **Opéra**, **Montparnasse** and along the Boulevards.

The *Morris* columns erected in many of the city streets are covered with posters telling passers-by what's on in the capital's theatres.

Two kiosks sell reduced-price seats for performances in the evening of the day on which you book – on the west side of the Madeleine (8e) and on the mall between the Montparnasse Tower (14e) and the railway station of the same name. (*Both these kiosks are open Tuesdays to Saturdays 12.30pm to 8pm, and Sundays 12.30pm to 4pm*).

SPORT

The **Parc des Princes**, the new **Stade de France**, **Palais Omnisports de Paris-Bercy**, stadiums such as **Charlety** and **Pierre-de-Coubertin**, the **Roland-Garros** tennis club and the **Halle Carpentier** are all used for top-level sports competitions open to the public. On the occasion of the World Football Cup, the **Grand Stade de France** opened. With is ultra modern design, boasting the largest seating capacity of any stadium, it offers a venue for major sporting events as well as concerts.

In addition to the numerous sports amenities, there are many places that are ideal for **running**: parks (**Parc Monceau**, 8e, **Parc Montsouris**, 14e; **Parc André-Citroën**, **Parc Georges-Brassens**, 15e, **Parc des Buttes-Chaumont**, 19e), the banks of the Seine, Allée des Cygnes beneath the Bir-Hakeim Bridge or woods such as **Bois de Boulogne** and **Bois de Vincennes**.

If you simply wish to walk and discover Paris at your own pace, try the **Promenade Plantée**, a 4.5km long walk on the former route of the Bastille-suburban railway line.

The **Aquaboulevard** at 4 rue Louis-Armand (*métro* Balard, RER boulevard Victor) is a vast complex with **water sports and leisure pools, tennis courts, bowling alley** and **gym** (busy on Wednesdays because there is no school on that day, and at weekends). For further information on sports amenities or forthcoming sports events, contact Allô-Sports, ☎ 0802 00 75 75; or www.paris-web.com

The Palais Omnisports de Paris-Bercy, on the east of the city.

THE BASICS

Before You Go

Visitors entering France should have a full passport, valid to cover the period in which they will be travelling. No visa is required for members of EU countries or US and Canadian citizens, but visitors from Australia and New Zealand may require an entry visa. This can be readily obtained from the French Embassies and Consulates in the home country.

No vaccinations are necessary.

Getting There

Flights leave from all over the world for the two destinations in Paris – Orly and Roissy-Charles-de-Gaulle – and are organized by both schedule and charter airlines.

Eurostar carries passengers from London via the Channel Tunnel to Paris in three hours, while Motorail will carry you and your car.

Several ferry companies carry cars and passengers across the Channel, with the quickest journeys being between Dover/Calais, and Folkestone/Boulogne. The hovercraft is even faster, crossing from Dover to Calais in just 35 minutes.

An efficient railway service connects the ports and Paris for foot passengers, and there are high-speed trains to Paris from many European cities. There are also coach services throughout Europe, as well as between London and Paris. If you plan to travel in the peak summer holiday period, or during Christmas, Easter or Whitsun, be sure to book well in advance.

Arriving

Air France operates a regular coach service between Roissy-CDG and Paris (Porte Maillot and Place de L'Étoile) every 15–20 mins, from 6am–11pm, and an RER (line B3) train service runs from 6.30am–11.50pm. There is also a bus which leaves for Paris-Opéra (Rue Scribe) every 15 minutes from 6am–11pm.

From Orly Airport the Air France coach leaves for Les Invalides every 12 minutes from 5.50am–11pm, and Orly Rail (line C2) runs from 5.35am–11.17pm. A bus service goes into Paris (Denfert-Rochereau) from 6.30am–11.30pm, leaving every 13 minutes. There is also a new link from Orly to the centre of Paris on the RER (line B), called Orly VAL.

Taxis are available from the

airports into the city (about 30.5€ from CDG and 22.9€ from Orly), and there is an additional tax supplement to be paid from these points.

There is no limit on the importation into Paris of tax-paid goods bought in an EU country, provided they are for personal consumption, with the exception of alcohol and tobacco which have fixed limits governing them.

Climbing one of the many stepped streets in Montmartre.

A-Z

Accidents and Breakdowns

A red warning triangle must be carried by cars towing a caravan or a trailer, in case of breakdown. While this is not compulsory for non-towing cars with hazard warning lights, it is strongly recommended. Fully comprehensive insurance is advisable, and motoring organizations recommend that you carry a green card, although this is no longer a legal requirement.

On *autoroutes* there are orange emergency telephones every 2 km (1.25 miles), and assistance is charged at a Government-fixed rate. Motorists can only call the police or the official breakdown service operating in that area, and not their own breakdown company. This also applies on the Paris *périphérique*.

Check with your insurance company before leaving for Paris what you should do in case of an accident. Generally, if an accident happens and nobody is hurt, a form *Constat*

à l'Amiable should be completed with full details. This must be signed by both parties, and sent off to the relevant insurers. Where someone is injured in a road accident, contact the Medical Emergency Service (*Samu*) on ☎ 15. The Fire Brigade is on ☎ 18 and the Police on ☎ 17.

Accommodation

See also **p.93**

The *Michelin Red Guides Paris* and *France* list a selection of hotels in Paris. They range from the modest to the extravagantly luxurious, and there are several *Café-Couette* in the city which offer bed and breakfast accommodation. An average comfortable hotel will cost around 91-122€ for two, with breakfast charged on top; an extra 30 per cent is usually added on for a third bed.

Many Paris hotels offer special break deals out of season, and details may be obtained by sending a SAE to the French Government

Tourist Office (*see* **Tourist Information Offices**). The tourist office also provides a full list of accommodation.

Young people looking for low-budget accommodation in Paris can get information from the **Centre International de Séjours à Paris**, 6 ave Maurice-Ravel, 12e ☎ 01 44 75 60 00, or 17 bd Kellerman, 13e ☎ 01 44 16 37 38. There are youth hostels run by the **Ligue F.U.A.J**, 67 rue Vergniaud, 13e ☎ 01 55 25 35 20.

There are also four youth hostels belonging to the YHA, known in France as the **Auberges de Jeunesse**:
Auberge Jules Ferry,
8 bd Jules Ferry, 75011 Paris
☎ 01 43 57 55 60
Auberge le d'Artagnan,
80 rue Vitruve, 75020 Paris
☎ 01 40 32 34 56
Auberge Cité des Sciences,
24 rue des 7 Arpents,
93310 Le Pré-Saint-Gervais
☎ 01 48 43 24 11
Auberge Leo Lagrange,
107 rue Martre, 92110 Clichy
☎ 01 41 27 26 90

MIJE youth hostels ☎ 01 42 74 23 45, have three 17C mansions in the heart of the Marais, and welcome the 18-30-year-old group on a limited budget who don't mind dormitories.

Banks

Opening hours are: 9am–noon, 2–4pm, weekdays, and banks are closed either on Mondays or Saturdays. They also close early on the day before a bank holiday.

Banks exchange travellers' cheques, and most have cash dispensers which accept international credit cards. A passport is necessary when cashing cheques in a bank. Some banks, but not all, will change money (*see also* **Money**).

Bicycles

The Parisian traffic makes cycling very dangerous, and it is not recommended. However, on Sundays some areas of central Paris are closed to motor vehicles making cycling more enjoyable.

Bicycles can be hired at the Maison de la roue libre, 95 bis, rue Rambuteau (near the Forum des Halles). The major railway stations also rent out bicycles which can then be returned to different stations.

Books

Here is a list of suggested reading to enhance your stay in Paris:
Balzac, Honoré de *Le Père Goriot* and *La Cousine Bette*
Beauvoir, Simone de *The Prime of Life*

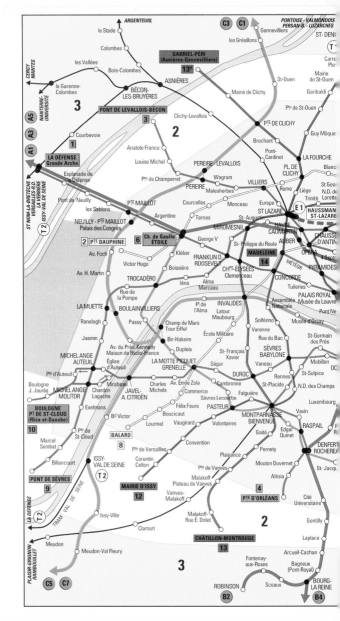

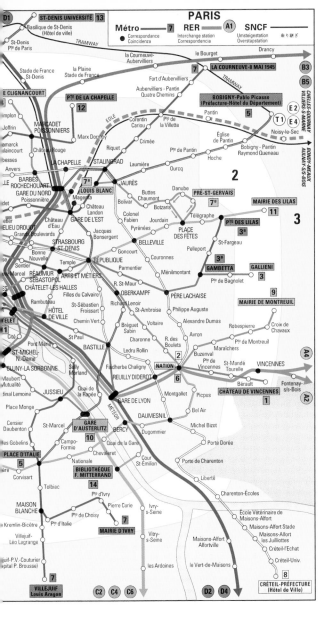

Cole, Robert *A Traveller's History of Paris*

Le Gallienne, Richard *From a Paris Garret*

Gibbings, Robert *Trumpets from Montparnasse*

Hemingway, Ernest *A Moveable Feast*

Hibbert, Christopher *The French Revolution*

Horne, Alastair *The Fall of Paris: The Siege and the Commune 1870–71*

Hugo, Victor *Les Misérables*

Littlewood, Ian *Paris: A Literary Companion* J

Orwell, George *Down and Out in Paris and London*

Tannahill, Reay, ed. *Paris in the Revolution: A Collection of Eye-Witness Accounts*

Wiser, Willliam *The Crazy Years: Paris in the Twenties*

Zola, Emile *Nana*

Camping

There is only one site in the city itself: **Camping Île de France**, allée du Bord-de-l'Eau, 16e ☎ 01 45 24 30 00, in the Bois de Boulogne next to the Seine, between the Pont de Puteaux and Pont de Suresnes. For information on sites around Paris, contact the **Camping Club de France**, 218 bd St-Germain, 7e ☎ 01 45 48 30 03; or **Fédération Française de Camping Caravaning**, 78 rue de Rivoli, 4e ☎ 01 42 72 84 08.

Car Hire

Paris is well stocked with car-hire agencies, and there are outlets at airports, air terminals and railway stations, as well as in the city centre. Airlines and tour operators offer fly/drive arrangements, and car hire in conjunction with train travel is available from French Railways.

Weekly rates with unlimited mileage is the best deal; these include collision damage waiver, personal accident insurance and local tax, and can be booked from any country. The lower age limit is 18, but few international companies hire to drivers under 20, 21, or even 23.

Drivers must have held their full licence for at least a year. With the exception of Avis, there is an upper age limit of 60–65. Unless paying by credit card a substantial cash deposit is required, but full details of the different hire schemes can be obtained from tourist offices. *See also* **Accidents and Breakdowns,** and **Tourist Information Offices**

Children

There are plenty of activities and entertainments for children in Paris, from zoos to huge playgrounds and special museums, and, of course,

Disneyland and Parc Astérix. Parisians usually welcome children, and expect them to be included in family groups in restaurants and hotels.

Babysitting agencies can provide English-speaking minders: A baba, ☎ 01 45 49 46 46 (8am–10pm daily); Baby Sitting Services ☎ 01 46 21 33 16; Kid Services ☎ 01 42 61 90 00. Prices include hourly fee plus agency fee and taxi.

Clothing

Comfortable casual clothing is accepted almost everywhere in Paris, but more formal dress is expected at some restaurants, in theatres and casinos, and at the opera. Spring and autumn evenings can be chilly, and an extra sweater or jacket is recommended.

Most French clothing measurements are standard throughout Europe but different from those in the UK. The following are examples:

Dress Sizes

UK	8	10	12	14	16	18
France	36	38	40	42	44	46
US	6	8	10	12	14	16

Men's Suits

UK/US	36	38	40	42	44	46
France	46	48	50	52	54	56

Men's Shirts

UK/US	14	14.5	15	15.5	16	16.5	17
France	36	37	38	39/40	41	42	43

Men's Shoes

UK	7	7.5	8.5	9.5	10.5	11
France	41	42	43	44	45	46
US	8	8.5	9.5	10.5	11.5	12

Women's Shoes

UK	4.5	5	5.5	6	6.5	7
France	37	38	38	39	39	40
US	6	6.5	7	7.5	8	8.5

At night when the boats' spotlights illuminate the majestic façades of the old hôtels, and highlight the decorative bridges and famous monuments, the trip is even more evocative!

Complaints

Complaints about taxis should be addressed to: Service Taxi – Préfecture de Police, 36 rue des Morillons – 75015 Paris. ☎ 01 45 31 14 80. At a hotel or restaurant make your complaint in a calm manner to the manager.

Consulates

Embassies and consulates can be found at the following addresses:

British Consulate
16, rue d'Anjou, 75008 Paris.
☎ 01 44 51 31 02

British Embassy
35 rue du Faubourg St-Honoré, 75008 Paris ☎ 01 44 51 31 00

Australian Embassy and Consulate
4 rue Jean-Rey, 75015 Paris.
☎ 01 40 59 33 00

Canadian Embassy and Consulate
35 avenue Montaigne, 75008 Paris ☎ 01 44 43 29 00

Irish Embassy
4 rue Rude, 75016 Paris.
☎ 01 44 17 67 00

New Zealand Embassy
7 ter Rue Léonard-de-Vinci, 75016 Paris ☎ 01 45 00 24 11

American Consulate
2 rue St-Florentin, 75008 Paris
☎ 08 36 70 14 88

American Embassy
2 avenue Gabriel, 75008 Paris
☎ 01 43 12 22 22

Crime

As is increasingly the case in big cities the world over, pick-pockets operate on the *métro*, in buses, and at many busy places – especially tourist attractions. The best advice is to be aware at all times, carry as little money, and as few credit cards as possible, and leave any valuables in the hotel safe. Never leave your car unlocked, and hide away or remove items of value.

If you have anything stolen, report it immediately to the nearest police station (*Commissariat de Police*), and collect a report so that you can make an insurance claim. Stolen passports should be reported to your Consulate or Embassy at once.

Disabled Visitors

The *Michelin Red Guide France* and *Michelin Guide Camping and Caravaning* indicate which hotels and camp sites have facilities for disabled visitors. You can also get information on Minitel 3615 HANDITEL (*see also* **Tourist Information Offices**).

'Access Project' at 39 Bradley Gardens, West Ealing, London W13 8HE offers a free English-language copy of *Access Paris* which provides well-researched information for the disabled visitor to Paris. Also in Britain, RADAR, at 12 City Forum, 250 City Road, London EC1V 8AF ☎ (020) 7250 3222, publishes factsheets with accommodation overseas for the disabled traveller.

Driving

Driving in Paris (on the right-hand side) can be a terrifying experience which is best left to the experts. If you must take your car through the capital, or are driving a hire car, make sure that you are very familiar with the rules of the road, and are clear about the route you are taking.

Drivers should carry a full national driving licence (nationals of EC countries) or an international one (nationals of non-EC countries), insurance documents including a green card (no longer compulsory for EU members but strongly recommended), registration papers for the car, and a nationality sticker for the rear of the car.

Headlight beams should be adjusted for right-hand drive, and a red warning triangle must be carried unless there are hazard warning lights on the car; you should also have a spare set of light bulbs.

Wherever possible use the ring road (the *périphérique*) instead of driving across the city. New, stricter parking regulations are now in force in Paris, and many streets are no-parking zones. However, in August parking is free on many roads. The minimum age for driving in France is 18. For general traffic information contact Allô Information Voirie on ☎ 01 40 28 73 73. *See also* **Accidents and Breakdowns**

Electric Current

The voltage in Paris – including campsites – is usually 220V. Plugs and sockets do vary, but adaptors are generally required.

The Arc de Triomphe at night.

Emergencies

For an emergency requiring:
Police ☎ 17, **Fire Brigade**
(Pompiers) ☎ 18, and
Ambulance (Samu) ☎ 15.
The Operator's number is 13,
and Directory Enquiries is 12.
Paris has an anti-poison centre:
☎ 01 40 05 48 48, and advice
on other urgent medical
conditions is available on:
☎ 01 47 07 77 77.
In emergencies, the Consulate
or Embassy might offer limited
help. *See* **Consulates**

Etiquette

As in most places in the world,
it is considered polite and
respectful to cover up decently
in churches, museums, and
theatres etc. The French are a
formal people, shaking hands
when they meet and address-
ing each other correctly by
their title when they are not
over familiar. Thus 'M'sieur
l'agent' is the right way to
address a police officer, and
'Bonjour Madame/Monsieur'
should begin any conversation
with a shopkeeper, post office
clerk or hotel desk staff, etc.

Excursions

Tours to places of interest both
in Paris and within easy driving
distance are many and varied.
Riverboats, including the huge
bateaux-mouches, offer an atmospheric trip along the Seine,
with their glass roofs for cold
or wet days, and the evening
boat tours show Paris under
floodlight.

Information can be found at
**Espace du Tourisme d'Ile-de-
France**, Le Carrousel du
Louvre, 99 rue de Rivoli, 1er
☎ 0803 81 80 00 (multilingual
information service, 10am-7pm
daily); **Cityrama Excursions** at
4 Place des Pyramides, Paris 1e,
☎ 01 44 55 61 12; and **Paris
Vision** at 214 rue de Rivoli,
Paris 1e, ☎ 01 42 60 30 01.

The **Opentour** bus tour lasts
2 hours and includes a com-
mentary in English. You can
get on or off at any of the 21
stops and the pass is valid for
two consecutive days. You can
buy a pass from your hotel or
at the Tourist Office.

There are also listings
magazines, such as *Pariscope*
and *Officiel des Spectacles* .

Health

UK nationals should carry a
Form E111 (forms available
from post offices) which is
produced by the Department
of Health, and which entitles
the holder to free urgent
treatment for accident or
illness in EU countries. The
treatment will have to be paid
for but can be reclaimed later.
All foreign nationals are

advised to take out comprehensive insurance cover, and to keep any bills, receipts and invoices to support any claim.

Lists of doctors can be obtained from hotels, chemists or police stations, and first aid and medical advice is also available at pharmacies (look out for the green cross). The latter are generally open from 2–7.30pm, Monday, 9am–7.30pm, Tuesday to Saturday, and those which are open late or on Sundays display notices on their doors. The **Pharmacie Dhéry** at 84, avenue des Champs-Élysées is open 24 hours a day, ☎ 01 45 62 02 41.

Internet

There is no shortage of web cafés in Paris. If browsing the net around the clock is your thing, head for **easyEverything** (37 bd Sebastopol) which has 375 computers and is open 24hr a day, 7 days a week.

Many museums have their own web site, which you may wish to check out before going. The Paris Tourist Office website, **www.paris-touristoffice.com**, has a number of links indicating museums, restaurants, hotels etc.

Language

Although English may be

Good morning / Bonjour
Goodbye / Au revoir
Yes/no / Oui/non
Please/thank you / S'il vous plaît/merci
Sorry / Pardon
Do you speak English? / Parlez-vous anglais?
I want to buy / Je voudrais acheter
How much is it? / Quel est le prix?
The bill, please / L'addition, s'il vous plaît
I'd like a booklet of tickets / Je voudrais un carnet de tickets
Is service included? / Le service est compris?
Black espresso / Un café or un express
White coffee / Un café au lait/crème
Fresh lemon/orange juice / Un Citron pressé/une orange pressée
A bottled beer / Une bouteille de bière
A draught beer / Une bière pression

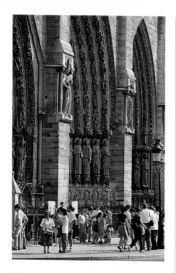

Entrance to Notre-Dame.

spoken more widely nowadays, you should try to speak in French. Do not assume you will be understood if you ask a question in English. It is a good idea to take a crash or refresher course before going to Paris. Elsewhere in France, your efforts will be appreciated, and even a few simple expressions are often warmly received.

Lost Property

If you lose anything whilst on the move in Paris, contact the Bureau des Objets Trouvés at 36 rue des Morillons, 15e,

Métro Convention, ☎ 01 55 76 20 00. Airports and major railway stations have their own lost property offices, and if something goes missing in your hotel, check with the front desk and hotel security.

Should you lose any travel documents, contact the police, and in the event of a passport going missing, inform your Embassy or Consulate immediately (*see* **Consulates**). Lost or stolen travellers' cheques and credit cards should be reported immediately to the issuing company with a list of numbers, and the police should also be informed.

Maps

Michelin Paris Plan **No 11** covers the city, with street maps and useful information and addresses, together with maps **Nos 10** and **12**. *Michelin Paris Transport* **No 9** covers bus, *métro*, RER and taxis within Paris. For those who wish to carry as little as possible, get the distinctive orange '*plan poche Paris*' (pocket map). The *Michelin Green Guide Paris* contains full details of the main sights and attractions within Paris, together with detailed maps. The complete range of Michelin guides and maps is available from the Boutique, 32 avenue de l'Opéra, Paris 75002.

Paris is divided into 20 *arrondissements* within the Boulevard Périphérique, and the postcode of an address will indicate which *arrondissement* it is in, e.g. 5e. *See also* **Tourist Information Offices**

Michelin on the Net:
www.ViaMichelin.com
This route-planning service covers all of Europe. Options allow you to choose a route and these are updated three-times weekly, integrating on-going road-works, etc. The descriptions include distances and travelling times between towns, selected hotels and restaurants.

Money

The French franc has been

The modern shopping centre of Forum des Halles.

replaced by the **euro** (€) the common currency for member countries of the European Community. Money conversions are now a thing of the past for nationals from the EC (except for the British, Danes and Norwegians).

The euro is divided into 100 cents, with 5, 10, 20, 50, 100, 200 and 500 euro notes, as well as coins worth 1 and 2 euros, and 1, 2, 5, 10, 20 and 50 cents. As a guide, 1 € = 6.56 francs (62p).

There are no restrictions on the amount of currency visitors can take into France, but perhaps the safest way to carry large amounts of money is in travellers' cheques which are widely accepted. Bureaux de change are found at airports, terminals, larger railway stations in popular tourist areas, and at banks. Cash dispensers accepting foreign credit cards are found throughout the city.

Exchange rates vary, so it pays to shop around. In the city centre there are minimum change banks offering good rates, often without commission charges. American Express, Carte Bleue (Visa/Barclaycard), Diners Club and Eurocard (Mastercard/Access) are widely accepted in shops, hotels and restaurants, motorways, petrol stations and many hypermarkets.

Always check the amount which appears on the receipt, and note that in France there is usually a comma rather than a decimal point between euros and cents.

Newspapers

A very wide range of foreign dailies, weeklies and monthlies arrive on Paris news-stands on the day of publication, and an excellent place to buy them is at W H Smith, 248 rue de Rivoli, 1e. You can buy papers and magazines at pavement news kiosks, bookshops and drugstores. French daily newspapers include *Le Monde*, *Le Figaro*, and *Libération*.

Opening Hours

The big stores and larger shops are generally open from 9am–6.30/7.30pm, Monday to Saturday. Some food shops open on Sunday mornings – bakers, for example – and close on Mondays, and they may close from noon–2pm for lunch. Opening hours are usually 9am–7pm, while hypermarkets stay open until 9pm or 10pm.

Chemists are generally open 2–7.30pm Monday, 9am–7.30pm Tuesday to Saturday; some open later and

on Sundays. Gendarmeries will give you their addresses (*see also* **Banks** and **Post Offices**).

Museums and monuments are open from 10am–5/6pm, and closing day is often Tuesday.

Photography

There are facilities for fast processing throughout the city. Before taking photographs in museums and art galleries it is wise to check with staff as photography is usually restricted in these places.

In some instances hand-held cameras are admitted free, while payment is required for tripods, and flashes are forbidden.

Police

French police wear a dark blue uniform and a flat cap. They are addressed as 'Monsieur l'Agent', and in emergencies can be contacted on ☎ 17. Police can impose and collect on-the-spot fines for drivers who violate traffic regulations.

Post Offices

Post offices are open Monday to Friday, 8am–7pm, and Saturday 8am–noon. Some are also open at other times but only offer a limited service, while the post office at 52 rue du Louvre is open 24 hours a day, every day; stamps are also available from newsagents and tobacconists.

Poste restante mail should be sent to the person at Poste Restante, Poste Centrale, Paris, with an *arrondissement* number (*see* **Maps**), and a passport should be taken along as proof of identity when collecting any poste restante mail.

Public Holidays

New Year's Day: 1 January
Easter Sunday and Monday (*Pâques*)
Labour Day: 1 May
VE Day: 8 May
Ascension Day: 40 days after Easter
Whitsun (*Pentecôte*): 7th Sunday and Monday after Easter
Bastille Day: 14 July
Assumption Day: 15 August
All Saints' Day (*Toussaint*): 1 November
Remembrance Day: 11 November
Christmas Day: 25 December

Religion

France is largely a Catholic country, but all the main religions are represented in Paris. The following are the chief ones:
St George's Anglican Church 7 rue Auguste-Vacquerie, 16e. ☎ 01 47 20 22 51

View from the Georges-Pompidou Centre towards Montmartre.

Church of Scotland 17 rue Bayard, 8e. ☎ 01 48 78 47 94
American Church 65 quai d'Orsay, 7e. ☎ 01 40 62 05 00
Liberal Synagogue 24 rue Copernic, 16e. ☎ 01 47 04 37 27
Great Synagogue 44 rue de la Victoire. ☎ 01 45 26 95 36 *or* 17 rue St-Georges, 9e. ☎ 01 40 82 26 26
Greek Cathedral of St-Etienne 7 rue Georges Bizet 16e.
La Mosquée 39 rue Geoffroy-St-Hilaire, 5e.

Smoking

Tabacs, licensed tobacconists displaying red diamond-shaped signs, sell cigarettes and pipe tobacco, but these are also on sale at drugstores and some restaurants and bars.

Telephones

Important: Most public telephones in Paris take phonecards (*télécarte*) which can be bought from post offices, tobacconists, newsagents, and at outlets advertized on telephone booths.

To call abroad from Paris, dial 00 and wait until the continuous tone recurs, then dial 44 plus STD code (minus first 0) followed by the number for the UK, 61 for Australia, 1 for Canada and the USA, 64 for New Zealand and 353 for Eire.

Cheap rates with up to 65 per cent extra time are between 9pm–8am, Monday to Friday, and at weekends from noon on Saturday. Calls can be received at phone boxes with the blue bell sign.

Emergency numbers

Fire 18; Police 17; Ambulance (Samu) 15; Operator 13; Directory Enquiries 12. For international enquiries dial 19 33 12 plus country code.

Minitel The French Telecom videotex offers information (via Minitel terminals, found in many hotels, post offices and some petrol stations) which is of interest to visitors. They include:

3614 ED electronic services in English
3615 TCAMP Camping information
3615 MÉTÉO Weather
3615 MICHELIN Michelin tourist/route information.

Time Difference

French standard time is GMT plus one hour. French summer time begins on the last Sunday in March at 2am when the clocks go forward an hour (the same day as British Summer Time), and ends on the last Sunday in September at 3am when the clocks go back (one month before BST ends).

Tipping

In Paris a 15 per cent service charge is usually included in the bill at hotels and restaurants, so there is no need to leave a tip, although if you pay by cash it is considered polite to leave the small change or up to 5 per cent for the waiter. Ask if you are not sure whether or not service has been included.

Public lavatory attendants with saucers may be happy with a few coins, but sometimes the price is displayed and is not negotiable. Tipping of 15 per cent is normal for taxi drivers, but not obligatory.

Toilets

Public conveniences can be found at railway stations, in public buildings and in department stores.

Tourist Information Offices

The French Government Tourist Office is an excellent first source of information on everything from where to stay in Paris to what to do on wet days.

Offices are at the following addresses:

UK 178 Piccadilly, London W1V 0AL ☎ 0891 44123.

Australia Kindersley House, 33 Bligh Street, Sydney, NSW 2000.

Canada 1981 Avenue McGill College, Suite 490, Esso Tower, Montreal, Quebec, H3 A2 W9.

USA 610 Fifth Avenue, New York 10020.

At the Accueil de France tourist office at 127 avenue Champs-Élysées, English-speaking staff will make hotel bookings for personal callers between 9am–8pm daily except 1 May. The offices are well stocked with leaflets providing information on excursions, transport, entertainment, facilities for the disabled, and exhibitions, as well as accommodation and restaurants. Guide books and maps are also for sale.

Before arriving, you can visit the official website: **www.paris-touristoffice.com**

The **Gare de Lyon** railway station also has a tourist office open daily (not Sundays or Bank Holidays) from 8am-8pm.

From May to September there is a tourist office at the Tour Eiffel (11am-6pm).

France Tourisme, 33 quai des Grands-Augustins, 6e, has a website, **www.francetourisme.fr** which also provides a lot of useful information (open daily 7am-9pm).

Transport

Paris is small and compact, with plenty of sightseeing on foot, but in order to make the most of a short stay the *métro* is a superb alternative. It is an efficient and safe form of transport, and in spite of the

Modern architecture in Paris.

fact that there are 370 stations – 87 of which are interchanges and no point in the capital is more than 500m (547yds) from a station – and 15 lines, it is very difficult to get lost. Stations are colour coded and signed, and lines are named after the last station in the direction you are travelling.

The RATP runs the inter-linked *métro*, bus and RER, and combined tickets cover journeys on all three services. There are four RER lines which serve the suburbs, and while there are few stops in the city centre, this is a very fast way of crossing town.

Métro tickets can be bought in booklets (*carnets*) of ten, and are also valid on the buses and the RER (the latter is subject to a special rate for the area). They are sold in *métro* booking halls, on buses, at tobacco counters, and at shops which show the sign RATP. Tourist tickets, *Paris Visite*, can be bought on production of a passport at larger *métro* stations, at Services Touris-tiques de la RATP, 55 quai des Grands Augustins, 6e, and at the Paris Tourist Office in the Champs-Élysées. The price varies according to the number of zones covered and the length of time for which it is issued (2, 3 or 5 days).

A Formula 1 ticket, valid for a single day, enables you to make an unlimited number of journeys on most of the public transport system in Paris.

Taxis cruise the streets of Paris, and are parked in ranks close to road junctions and other frequented points under a *Tête de Station* sign. They may also be hailed in the street when the white light is showing on the roof, and depending on the time of day and the zone it is in, a different coloured light will show inside to indicate the rate of charge. An extra charge is made for awkward and heavy luggage, for a fourth person, and for taxis hailed from station forecourts and airport terminals (*see also* **Arriving**).
Taxis bleus ☎ 01 49 63 10 10
Alpha-Taxis ☎ 01 45 85 85 85
Taxis G7 ☎ 01 47 39 47 39
Artaxi ☎ 01 42 41 50 50

The **Batobus** is a summer river bus which runs a limited service between the Eiffel Tower and the Hôtel de Ville, with five stopping places.

Water

Water served in hotels and restaurants is perfectly safe to drink, as is tap water unless labelled *eau non potable* (not drinking water). If you want water with your meal, specify *eau minérale* .

INDEX

This index includes entries in both English (where used in the guide) and in French (*italics*).